If U are fighting through adversity . . .
If U need inspiration . . .
If U need a map to find your *why* . . .
If U simply want to read a personal development story that U cannot put down . . .
Grab this book. Trust me: U will want to share it with everyone U know!

> Frank Neal
> President
> La-Z-Boy Furniture Galleries of Arizona

Inspiring, compelling, and, most importantly, authentic. *From Me to U* shares real-life journeys of discovery and fulfillment while offering readers meaningful messages to improve their own situations.

> Matthew Fehling
> President and CEO
> Better Business Bureau Serving the Pacific Southwest

Jodi Low, through a straightforward, conversational approach, offers the reader insight into her decision making and focus on improving one's life with a positive, values-based concept. Her dedication to developing leaders while raising her daughters is a consistent refreshing theme and the sound advice she provides throughout will help each reader become a more effective leader.

> Dr. Christine Wilkinson
> Senior Vice President and Secretary of the University
> Arizona State University

The pages of *From Me to U* tell the story of perseverance, a deep heart to serve others, and how being additive to the world is just good business. Jodi's personal story blends beautifully with the journey U & Improved students take. Helping people find their own joy and greatness is Jodi's business plan, and the impact she makes in the world is incredible. Leaders from all industries could stand to lead more from the heart, and *From Me to U* gives the inspiration to start doing just that.

> Jeremy Kraut-Ordover
> Chief Development Officer
> Muscular Dystrophy Association

From Me to U

Lessons on Life, Leadership,
and Living Your Legacy

———————

JODI LOW

Founder and CEO
U & Improved

Writers of the Round Table Press
PO Box 1603, Deerfield, IL 60015
www.roundtablecompanies.com

Deerfield, IL

Editor: **Kelsey Schurer**
Design: **Sunny DiMartino**
Copyeditor: **Sheila Harris**
Proofreader: **Adrian Bumgarner**
Print and Digital Post Production: **Sunny DiMartino**

Printed in the United States of America

First Edition: November 2022
10 9 8 7 6 5 4 3 2 1

Library of Congress Cataloging-in-Publication Data
Low, Jodi.
From me to u / Jodi Low.—1st ed. p. cm.
ISBN Paperback: 978-1-61066-101-0
ISBN Digital: 978-1-61066-102-7
Library of Congress Control Number: 2022917590

Writers of the Round Table Press and the logo
are trademarks of Writers of the Round Table, Inc.

To the two best gifts I have ever received:

Alexandra Elisabeth *and* **Iliana Elise**

This book, and my life, is dedicated to the two of U.

The longest journey U will ever take in your life is eighteen inches . . . from your head to your heart. Always lead, live, and love from those beautiful hearts of yours.

I love U and will forever be your biggest, raving fan. Live big, live boldly, and live all in.

I am so proud of U, always and forever,

Your Mommy

Contents

Introduction

A young man in his late thirties with thick, wavy brown hair, boot-cut jeans, tan suede tennis shoes, and an intense look on his face—we'll call him Mr. Smith—jumps up out of his chair.

"I am Mr. Smith!" he belts out across a room of some two hundred people.

"I am POWERFUL!"

"I am CONFIDENT!"

"I . . . AM . . . A . . . LEADER!!"

A roar rises from the nineteen other people seated in a semicircle around him. From the moment he pounced out of his chair, they've been clapping like he's their long-lost brother and he just won a billion dollars. By the time he hits the word *leader*, the pillowy hotel conference room walls are vibrating from the thunderous applause and howls of support that emanate across the entire room. Mr. Smith is dancing now, his arms above his head, jazz hands spread. The energy in the room is through the roof.

And here it comes. Every time I see this scene unfold, the tears come in a steady stream. I reach for a Kleenex, which isn't hard considering the room is strewn with tissue boxes. They're everywhere. On the floor, under the seats, lined along the trainers' desk at the front of the room. I always say I should have bought stock in Kleenex because, goodness knows, I single-handedly keep them in business.

How did I get here? How did I go from a happy-go-lucky little girl, who was raised primarily by her equally happy-go-lucky father, to having my dreams come true in the form of a room exploding with enthusiasm? How did I survive a divorce—okay, two divorces—a disastrous partnership and . . . and . . .

Well, as my grandfather used to say, paraphrasing the works of the great Greek philosopher Socrates, "I know nothing, but because I DO know I know nothing, I know more."

That's how I did it. Throughout my wild and worthy life, I knew that every step of the journey was a lesson. Every setback was a chance for me to learn and grow. And every time I conquered one of those setbacks, I stood taller and grew stronger. And when I turned my head to look behind me, I saw that the number of people who had my back kept multiplying. It was as if my heart knew all along the direction I needed to go.

And it was my heart that led me to the decision to finally write this book back in the crazy and tumultuous year of 2020.

As a corporate trainer, peak-performance coach, inspirational speaker, and founder of U & Improved—an experiential leadership and personal-development training company—I often share glimpses of my personal story. Time and again, I have had people approach me after a speaking engagement or class and say, "Wow, you seem so together. I would have never thought you went through all of that," or simply, "I don't know how you do it."

Those exact comments spurred me on to write this book.

To share with you not just the *hows* but also the *whys* of building U & Improved.

I wrote this book for you, or as I prefer to write, U. (I toyed with the idea of using U in lieu of *you* throughout this entire book, but my editor shook her head firmly against it.) The reason that the U is so important to me is that it has become a symbol of our unity in the human condition. My belief is that somewhere between U and I there is an us, and that our cumulative experiences in life may make us who we are, but they do not, and should not, define us. Our stories help us relate to one another, to bond and form lifelong, everlasting relationships.

And what I know is that in life, it's how you—yes, U—respond that makes all the difference.

In this book, I share personal stories about my life with the intent of sharing pivotal lessons I learned as I navigated my way through them. As I gained more wisdom from these experiences, I realized my level of joy correlated directly to how I *responded* to the situations and challenges that happened time and again. My responses were how I learned and grew, developed and evolved. And some things never change . . . just like you, I am still learning and evolving every day.

You'll notice as you read that the book is divided into four sections, based on the courses we offer at my company, U & Improved:

U the Leader challenges you to examine your mindset, how you think about and approach certain decisions and choices in your life.

U the Communicator offers a glimpse into the power of honest and authentic communication and putting relationships above self.

U the Warrior embraces the process of trust, both within yourself and with others, and examines how in order to follow your dreams, you must learn to trust your gut . . . and your tribe.

U the Samurai heightens your awareness of empathy, what it means to serve others, to hold firm to your anchor, and better the world one step at a time.

Each chapter within each section shares a personal story of mine and a *Dear U* reflection, wherein I share the lesson I took away from the experience and actionable guidance for how you might apply that lesson in your own life today.

Many of these life experiences occurred a long time ago, so I do ask you, dear reader, to please grant me a smidge of grace. Like yours, my memory is malleable (so much so that my brother lovingly refers to me as "the human Etch A Sketch"). However, please know that I did my very best in recounting each story from the purest place, with the most loving heart, and from the very best of my memory. And fair warning: let that grace also extend to my use of foul language within these pages. Yes, I know it's unladylike to curse. (My grandmother would certainly agree with this!) But the truth is I am an insane lover of language; I absolutely obsess over words. And for me, words carry a lot of power, passion, and energy. And sometimes, in my life and in my writing, no other words elicit exactly how I feel quite like a perfectly placed f-bomb does. If it offends you, my apologies in advance. However, authenticity is one of my core values and in this book, I am 100 percent unabashedly myself.

Finally, each person in this book has taught me something powerful and has shaped the trajectory of my life. In the spirit of protecting their privacy, I have changed some names of those who have nudged these lessons to the surface. While many of these stories were painful to live through and difficult to recount, I am truly grateful to every person who has entered, and perhaps exited, my life. Every interaction with the people mentioned between these pages has been written from my perspective on the story and the lesson I learned from the experience. I recognize, too, that each person present in this book also has their own story to tell and their own lessons to learn. If I had to do it all over again, I wouldn't change a thing about these moments because each lesson was truly THAT valuable.

So as you sit there on the other side of these pages, whether you are a first-time entrepreneur looking to launch a business, a corporate executive looking to ignite or reignite your passion, a single parent searching for clarity and hope, or a college student just being introduced to the vast world of personal development, my sincerest hope is that when you read this book, you can take my stories, and their lessons, and apply them directly to YOUR life, no matter what age or phase of life you are in.

Perhaps by the time you close this book, you too will be jumping up and down and shouting, just like Mr. Smith did, ready to take on the next curveball that life throws at you. This time, you will have more tools in your tool belt, a heart wide open to new growth, and a deeper understanding of who you are and how you respond to challenges and experiences.

This invitation to a better U is the gift I wish to share within these pages.

From me to U,

the
Leader

———

CHAPTER ONE

Picking Up the Pieces

Sometimes good things fall apart so better things can fall together.
—Marilyn Monroe—

My second pregnancy was nothing like my first. It started out feeling pretty similar, but then things just shifted. I felt more tired, but that could easily have been because I was also chasing a toddler around this time. Because it felt different, I immediately assumed that I must be having a boy this go-around. I'm not sure where that bit of logic came from, but, hey, I was a naive, young mom and assumed a different pregnancy experience must equate to different genders . . . somehow.

We found out that we were indeed having a second girl, and I was thrilled. I would have been equally thrilled either way, but the idea of two girls—sisters—just seemed so magical to me. I didn't have a sister, or a mom, in my life, so the idea of sharing those moments of childhood—the giggles, the sleepovers, the puberty drama, the dating—seemed fun to share with a sister. I was elated that my oldest daughter would soon have a baby sister to grow up alongside her!

But, as mentioned, this pregnancy was different. CRAZY different. The initial difference I noticed was the cravings. With my first pregnancy, all I craved was meat—bacon, steak, hamburgers, liverwurst—but this time, it was ALL about the sweets! Chocolate, ice cream, sugar. I had to be very careful not to overindulge those pregnancy urges.

For the first two trimesters, things were going relatively smoothly, but when the third trimester rolled around, I noticed a strange red rash forming all over my belly. It itched and was so uncomfortable. Coupled with the heat of a typically brutal Arizona summer, I was miserable. I reached out to my obstetrician, who, upon examining me, let me know that what I was experiencing was called a PUPPP rash.

PUPPP. It sounded cute enough, but let me tell you, this was anything but cute. In hindsight, my belly looked like a giant COVID-19 cell with red, raised, itchy bumps covering my ginormous, rock-hard baby belly.

To add insult to injury (or more discomfort to an already miserable trimester), I also acquired something called *fifth disease*. I don't know why I tend to attract the most bizarre health scenarios, but I am certainly notorious for them, but more on that later . . . *This* seemingly bizarre ailment hit me like a freight train during that final trimester, in the month of June, in Arizona, nine whole weeks before I was due to deliver.

Fifth disease during pregnancy can create fever, headaches, and rashes, but the symptom that packed a punch for me was severe, unending joint pain. Thankfully, I have never experienced the pain of arthritis, but I can only imagine it must feel something like having fifth disease during pregnancy. *Everything* hurt. Every joint, every movement. Walking quickly became a sort of shuffle-slide, as actually bending my knees and walking was excruciating. Having a two-year-old to chase after and a home to manage made every chore exactly that—a CHORE. I remember the pain I felt pushing the grocery cart through the store, literally leaning on it for support as I shuffled down the aisles like an overweight harpooned seal just waiting to die. Okay, maybe a bit dramatic, but . . . not really. It freaking *sucked* and hurt like hell.

However, there was one thing I knew for sure. Despite all my ailments and fatigue, I couldn't wait to meet this second little angel of mine. And my sweet Alexandra was going to become a big sister soon! I was so excited to see them meet each other. My heart would explode with joy at the thought of how precious this sisterly relationship would be. Every bit of pain was more than worth the gift that was coming.

One blisteringly hot summer day in July, just a couple of weeks before my second daughter was to arrive, the proverbial shit hit the fan.

When I say it was hot out, it was hot. REALLY hot. It was late afternoon, and I had just returned home from one of the most painful days. My rash was out of control, creating itching and constant discomfort, but that was nothing compared to the joint pain. Every movement was a living nightmare. I had held on to the shopping cart for dear life that day, counting my lucky stars that there was finally an end in sight: only a couple more weeks of this agony and the pain would end.

When I arrived home from the grocery store, I walked into the front door and saw my husband, Mike, lying on the couch and working on his laptop. Now if you knew Mike, you would know that he was on his phone or laptop . . . *a lot.*

These were the very early days of social media. Facebook had just launched and was the big new buzz. I remember Mike telling me all about it and how he had connected with so many old friends that he hadn't been in contact with in years. It all seemed a little weird to me at the time. *Why would I want to connect with people from decades ago? If we were truly friends, wouldn't we have stayed connected all these years?* It did intrigue me though, and soon enough I found my first "Facebook friend," a dear friend from high school that I still keep in touch with today. My journey into social media began, months after my husband had been a part of it.

And that was so very Mike. He was always "in the know." What was new, what was happening, what was hot and trending. He loved being on the inside and being that pioneer discovering new ideas and opportunities.

And he loved people, and people loved him. They gravitated toward him with his charm and magnetic personality. He had more of a calm and quiet demeanor when you first met him, but you were quickly pulled into his fun-loving, easygoing, "everything is allllll good" vibe. He was just fun to be around, and he LOVED to stir things up, which was how he earned the nickname "the Swizzler." He loved to have fun and "mix things up," just like the swizzle stick in your favorite cocktail. With his charismatic charm, he always made sure everyone was having a good time.

But my husband wasn't the only one to draw you in with charm. Mike and I had one fur baby whom we adored. Boston, our sweet black lab, was our first "daughter." Technically, Boston was MY first daughter, as she and I were family before Mike and I began dating. So sweet, so loving, Boston would lie in the doorway of my daughter's nursery to make sure she was safe and protected. She was a beautiful, sweet spirit whom everyone loved. Every time I walked into the room, she would greet me with those gorgeous brown eyes and a tail wagging so fast I was sure it would wiggle right off one day. A mild-mannered black lab, she was a docile girl getting up in years, but still had all the love in the world for her "people." And I sure did love her, getting lots of cuddles and snuggle time in, even if there was a little human baby vying for my attention, with another one on the way. While he wasn't nearly the dog lover I was, my husband liked Boston. You just couldn't help but love this sweet girl.

Now, with a big dog comes big "droppings," and I don't know about you, but I don't know anyone who loves the job of picking up poop. In the undefined list of spousal "duties," no pun intended, this job fell into my column. It was no big deal, as I was always the poop-picker-upper for our childhood dogs, and being that Boston and I were a package deal entering this relationship, I was A-OK doing poop patrol.

But poop patrol, paying the bills, managing the house, washing all the laundry, and doing the cleaning and grocery shopping while still working daily in our business, raising our toddler, AND being so big and uncomfortably pregnant . . . it was getting tiresome.

Mike WAS great about getting the baby in the middle of the night when she was a newborn and needed to be fed and putting her down for naps when she was tired. And I sincerely appreciated that help and support. What I wasn't okay with was the obvious inequity that had developed. Any great relationship isn't 50/50, in my mind. A great relationship is 100/100, which means both people are 100 percent invested, committed, and giving of themself. All in. Always.

Lately, that 100/100 wasn't happening.

Mike was disconnected. Constantly focused on that damn laptop and his phone, so "busy" with "work." Yet, deep down, I knew the work he was doing. And Facebook wasn't work . . . period.

But back to this blistering summer day. Like always, Boston came to greet me when I walked inside our house, waiting for me to unload the bags I was carrying so she could get some love from Mom.

Meanwhile, my husband was lying on the couch, working on his laptop. I could see the infamous blue and white background of Facebook from his screen. He had muttered a quick hello, but seemed quite engrossed in his computer. So, as I unloaded the groceries from the car, I reminded him of how uncomfortable I was.

"Ugh, that sucks. Sorry, Turkey," he said.

(Yes, "Turkey." That was one of our pet names for each other. It came from us calling the baby a "Stinky Turkey" when she had a diaper explosion, and, somehow, that became a term of endearment we called one another. Weird, I know.)

He didn't even glance up from his screen.

Yeah, I felt the love.

But I reminded myself that he was probably busy and that no one enjoys hearing someone complain, so I did my best to quietly put the groceries away.

I couldn't help noticing, as I peered past the couch and out the sliding glass door, that the dog poop had yet to be picked up in the backyard. I had asked my husband on two different occasions earlier that week if he could please pick up the dog poop, and both times he simply said, "Sure," and yet the dog poop was still in the grass.

And in the gravel.

And on the patio.

Now, if you know me, you know I am a "get shit done" (another unintentional pun) kind of girl, so the fact that, after two requests, the poop was still roasting in the sun and hadn't been picked up was definitely irritating to me. I was itchy, achy, sweaty, exhausted, and hormonal—a recipe for disaster.

And the thought of asking him a third time really had me fired up. However, I remember consciously telling myself to ask kindly, one more time, and so I did . . .

"Hey, so I asked you to please pick up Boston's poop a couple of times, and it's still there. Can you please go out there and pick it up for me?"

For me. Really, was it "for me"? Or was it for us and any other human with nostrils and shoes they cared about . . .

There was a small pause. "Sure, Turks . . . no problem." I was sure that would be his response.

And then . . . his actual response.

"It's YOUR dog."

Oh.

My.

God.

My dog? MY DOG?? What about all the *we, us, 'til death do us part, we're in this together* stuff didn't he get? MY DOG?!

I was seething. If there had been literal fire coming out of my ears, I wouldn't have been surprised, although I am sure it was just the intense flames combusting off my nine-months-pregnant, rash-covered, beach-ball belly.

The words hung in the air. The deafening silence hung in the air, but only for a split second, before the click of his fingers hitting the keyboard brought me back to my reality.

I grabbed two plastic Target grocery bags and marched (okay, shuffled) outside. My head was spinning. As I placed one bag over my hand for a makeshift glove and used the other bag to collect my treasures, his words echoed in my ears. *It's YOUR dog.*

Did he not see me? Did he not get the concept of marriage? Yes, it was just dog poop. But it so wasn't. It was so much more.

With every piece of poop I picked up that afternoon, I kept thinking about his actions and his words and how they seemed to lack empathy, caring, and compassion. He could be such a loving and sweet guy, but what was this? Why was his behavior so disconnected and detached from his wife?

Something had shifted.

The man I knew and married was a fun-loving and *thoughtful* man. He would give little "just because" cards and gifts, plan a fun date night out to a great new restaurant that had just opened or to see the latest movie that everyone was anxiously awaiting. But since he had become a father, things had shifted. I couldn't put my finger on it (probably because my fingers were on pieces of dog shit), but I could feel it. Something . . . changed.

Of course, the biggest change was that we were parents. Parents of a gorgeous baby girl with another on the way. But more than that, I had changed. I was a mother now. And while I was doing what I felt was my best to be a loving wife, my main priority was my little Alexandra. Making sure she ate, and slept, and pooped, and laughed.

But Mike and I still saw friends, did backyard barbecues, date night every week . . . it wasn't like there was no connection or any kind of dismissal of one another. So what exactly about us had changed? I was stumped.

There's a story Mike's mom had told me numerous times. It was one of her "playlist tracks," as Mike referred to her stories that seemed to repeat quite often . . .

Mike's mom, Rose, would always have a huge grin on her face when she would talk about her beloved son. He was her one and only child, and if there was ever a mother who believed their child hung the moon, Rose believed it was most certainly her little Mikey. She would tell me stories of how he had so many natural gifts: his "golden arm" for baseball, his natural athletic talents on the football and basketball teams, how he was just a born entrepreneur. She "played" two "tracks" about Mike's entrepreneurial nature in his youth, both of which I still remember to this day.

When Mike was a little boy, Rose would give him the chore of clipping the hedges. She told me, proudly, that she wanted to instill the value of hard work in her son. Mike's chore was to trim the little stragglers that would pop up and even out the tops and sides, keeping them shipshape between visits from the landscaper. No big deal.

At the time, there was a pair of cool new sunglasses (I am assuming they were Vuarnet, because, well, the 1980s . . .) that he REALLY wanted. She told Mike that if he wanted them, he needed to earn part of the money to help pay for them. She would pay him ten dollars each time the hedges needed clipping. The hedges were his way to the promised land of '80s fashion, and he knew this.

But rather than clip the hedges himself, this budding entrepreneur had another idea. He called his buddy in the neighborhood, who also wanted to make a few bucks, and told him he would pay him five dollars to clip the front-yard hedges. The friend was thrilled, and so Mikey sat back, peering out the large bay window, watching his friend work while he counted his singles.

This entrepreneurial spirit didn't stop there. Rose would share the story about how Mikey had been hired by his father, who worked in agriculture and farming, to help pick the strawberry fields. He lasted half a day. Four hours. Done. Never went back.

"Yeah, Mom, that's never happening again," Mikey proclaimed.

"What do you mean, Mijito . . . your father thinks this would be a great summer job for you and you will learn a lot," Rose clamored.

"No way, Mom. Way too hot, way too much manual labor . . . not for me."

Those were his words, as the story went. Just a few hours in and he told his mom he was never going to work like that again, outside, sweating, his skin burning in the heat of the day.

"Mom, I will never work in that field again. The only time I will step foot in a strawberry field is when I own it."

Rose was so proud of her young entrepreneur. How sweet, and how remarkable, that he knew from such a young age that his calling was to own his own business one day.

———

Shuffling through the gravel with sweat dripping down my forehead and back, these unusual stories were swirling through my mind.

Was Mike really a budding entrepreneur since birth? Was he the gifted boy with a brilliant mind for business that his beaming mother loved to share about? Or was Mikey just . . . dare I say it . . . *lazy?*

When I started to think about our current state of running a business and raising our girls, I thought about my role in our marriage. I was obviously running around with my toddler, doing all the invisible labor of keeping the house up and keeping my family happy.

But I was also the one handling the labor of our business. I was making all the phone calls, including those super-fun cold calls and all the high-stakes sales calls. I was the one stuffing all the envelopes and mailing out all the marketing materials. I was the one handling all the accounting, keeping tabs on all the bills and all the numbers.

Mike was the "visionary." The "idea guy." The master puppeteer.

Was I just clipping the hedges for five dollars?

Oh . . . shit.

———

Time pressed on. The next few hot summer weeks dragged on at the same speed as me shuffling around the house, hanging on to any bits of cool AC that I could find. And on July 24th, our darling Iliana arrived, happy and healthy, with a full head of hair and a sweet face that made me giggle each time I looked into her deep-brown eyes. Life became even more full, and busier. But I was so happy. The girls were so precious. Seeing Alexandra so proud to be a big sister and so in love with her little Iliana was enough to make my heart melt.

Watching Mike with the girls was endearing. And just like the first go-around with Alexandra, he would get up to bring Iliana to me in the middle of the night so I could feed her, as it was tough to do after my second C-section. I so appreciated that. He would drive Alexandra around in the car when she just couldn't calm down enough to take her afternoon nap, and I would watch him sway Iliana from side to side to calm her down when she was getting fussy. I loved those little moments of seeing him with the girls. There was no doubt he adored them. And it certainly meant everything to me to experience that kind of support, especially when I was post-pregnancy. It felt good and right again. This reality was much nicer than the one I was thinking about as I picked up that poop in the Target bags. This was good.

Until it wasn't. Again.

Reality became all too real just six months later.

We were building our dream home and we needed to find a rental—something nearby that we could rent for twelve months while the home was being constructed and completed. This new home and new chapter with our girls was so exciting. And overwhelming.

When it came time to look for the rental, Iliana was still just a little bitty thing, and Alexandra was a busy toddler who was inquisitive and alert, and never, EVER wanted to take a nap lest she miss out on something.

Yet, as the time approached, Mike was busy, busy, busy on that laptop. It became apparent that, like most things, finding a rental would fall on me. I reached out to a friend who was a Realtor, arranging time to go look at some houses with him. Mike said he wasn't coming along; he trusted me to find a good place. He was going to stay back and work.

On the morning of the meeting with the Realtor, as I got ready, I assumed (my fault for assuming) that the girls would stay with Mike at home, so I wouldn't be schlepping a two-year-old and nine-month-old in and out of the Realtor's car, taking them through house after house, missing naps and meals and feedings and diaper changes and snacks. The logic in this seemed obvious to me. The girls needed to sleep and eat. Mike was staying at home, so he could handle watching over them while I found us a new home.

Wrong.

"What do you mean?" I said, shocked, staring at him as he sat on the couch. "You want me to take the girls with me all day to look at houses? What about naps, feeding them—"

He cut me off.

"You can handle it."

"Well, I know I CAN handle it, but why would I when you are going to be home? You can work on your laptop while they are both napping . . ."

I could feel the air shift in the room. He was getting enraged.

"WHY CAN'T YOU JUST HANDLE IT?"

Because I handle everything, I thought. Still, I stood my ground.

"Mike, are you kidding me right now? I am not doing this with a toddler and a baby if I don't absolutely have to! It makes no sense!"

He bolted off the couch. Within seconds, he was standing in front of me, his anger palpable between us. He grabbed my arms and squeezed. His grip constricting, I couldn't break free. He squeezed so hard, I screamed.

"What are you DOING??"

He let go and then walked around the arm of the couch. Full of rage, he took his middle finger and flicked me in the back of the neck with all his might.

Now, a flick in the neck doesn't seem as painful as you'd expect.

But oh, it hurt. It hurt so bad. And I am not talking about the physical pain of that flick or the grip marks and bruises he left on my upper arms.

I'm talking about my heart. It hurt. It was aching. I couldn't understand it. *What was happening?*

Ding-dong. The Realtor had arrived to pick me up. I quickly wiped my tears and answered through the door that I would be there in a minute. Then I scooped up my babies and left without a backward glance at my husband. Outside, I told the Realtor I needed to grab the car seats, and he kindly helped me install them in his car. I am certain he was just as shocked as I was that two little babies were coming with us, but there was no way I was leaving them with an enraged father.

I was getting us out of there.

———

That afternoon, Mike apologized. He always did.

"I'm really sorry, Turkey. I didn't mean to get so upset. You know how much I love you and the girls and appreciate all that you are doing."

He was always so heartfelt with his words, all the little instances of *babe* and *Turkey* and *I love you* and *I appreciate you*. He explained that he just had a lot to do and he, too, assumed just as I had assumed . . .

He assumed that I would be taking the girls with me. In a Realtor's car. To look at a half dozen homes all around the city. When they needed to eat. And nap. And . . .

Whatever. It wasn't exactly logical, but I accepted his apology, like I always did. And I believed another excuse I made for his behavior. He was stressed (so was I) by the busyness of two little kids, a pending move, getting a new home built, and running a business. I needed to let it slide (he would do the same for me, right?) and just forget about it.

But it was hard to forget. The bruises on my arms and the replay of that finger smacking the back of my neck . . . those images didn't go away.

I decided on a rental, and soon after, it was time to get the house cleaned out for the move to begin. There were so many boxes . . . boxes upon boxes upon boxes. I sat sprawled out on the floor late at night, after getting the girls to sleep, working into the wee hours of the morning so I could have some uninterrupted time, wrapping each glass and taping each box. Every spatula, every onesie, every tiny toy—I packed it. One after the other. Me. Myself. I. That was my moving team. My hands were so dry from all the paper and my eyes were so heavy from not sleeping.

And that same moving team did all the unpacking. We were strong, the three of us. Me, myself, and I were a team, and we worked for days on end, once again staying up into the early morning hours to get things set up while the babies slept. While their father slept. He had been working hard, you know. He was "beat." *I'm sure you are,* I thought to myself as I hung his shirts in the closet for him. *You must be simply . . . exhausted.*

I felt so alone.

I couldn't hide from this new reality. I couldn't pretend it didn't exist. The reality was that my husband was absent in almost every area of our marriage. The occasional times he helped out with our girls were far outweighed by every time I handled the bills, the household chores, and playing with our girls, not to mention all the work I put into building our business, too. He wasn't alone in the business. He had me. But I didn't have him. And every conversation about it, no matter how nicely I packaged it, was met with hostility and anger. He knew it was true. He knew he wasn't showing up for me. And ultimately, he was okay with it.

And in that moment, I continued to pack down my feelings, as I unpacked another box.

Dear U,

I was always told that the way a man treats his mother is the way he will treat his wife. As most of these clichés do, this one fell on deaf ears. Boy, I wish I had opened my eyes (and ears) more back then.

Just like me, U can easily miss those glaring signs, but if U take away anything from this story, let it be this: **When people show U who they are, believe them.**

It's not that people are inherently "bad" or "good." We all have faults and we all have strengths. However, there are certain aspects of relationships with people, whether romantic, professional, or otherwise, that will work for U and with U, and those that don't—the *dealbreakers*.

Looking back at my own life, though there were times when I was young and naive about the world, I have always had a sense of *knowing* and intuition. Like when you get goose bumps or your hair raises at the back of your neck. Whether it's a "good" or "bad" feeling is irrelevant. For me, when the goose bumps appear, I know it's the "right" thing and I need to pay attention to it, no matter what. During my divorce, I had that other kind of "knowing," the opposite of goose bumps. I knew that my life was NOT what I wanted it to be and that something was off. I also knew that I can't change other people to make my life better. They are who they are. Mike is who he is. The only person I can change . . . is me.

And the only person U can change is U.

Today, I get the honor of empowering people with a vast array of tools to do this inner work, but ultimately, the choice to pick up those tools and use them—to truly change and improve—lies within U.

So if U are ready to embrace these goose-bump moments, become aware of being unaware, and keep becoming your best, here's your game plan:

Trust your gut—it doesn't lie. Pay attention and don't just dismiss the wrong or hurtful behavior U may see or experience in your relationships. Truly seek to discover why this behavior doesn't work for U.

Keep pushing yourself to grow, to learn, and to be challenged. The power of self-reflection is immeasurable and it pays dividends throughout the rest of your life. If U see something that U are doing or becoming that U don't like, ask yourself what U can change within U, and then do it.

Demand the best of yourself. Ask yourself the tough questions: Am I happy? What brings me joy? What am I tolerating? What do I want the balance of my life to look like?

Run far away from the dealbreakers. They won't change, and U aren't doing yourself any favors by perpetuating a life that isn't working for U. Period.

Remember, dear reader, U deserve more. In fact, U deserve it all ... whatever *all* means for U. Get clear and go get it. Your time is now.

With love and gratitude,

CHAPTER TWO

D-Day

A woman is like a tea bag—only in hot water do you realize how strong she is.
—Eleanor Roosevelt—

I always knew that my dream was to one day be married with two or three children. And while I wasn't the girl who fantasized about the white dress and walking down the aisle, I just somehow knew that I am a relationship kind of a girl. I'm not exactly sure where that knowing or feeling came from. If I had to guess, it was a lot of after-school specials and too many reruns of *The Brady Bunch*. I knew that one day, I too would have that darling little family that every made-for-TV movie of the '80s depicted. And during my young adulthood I quickly realized I am not one who enjoys dating multiple people at once. I never even entertained the idea; it just always felt foreign to me. How could you date one guy on Thursday, another on Friday, and a third on Saturday? I saw friends who loved the dating scene, but for some reason, it just wasn't my jam.

For me, it was always about that one person. Loyalty and commitment were paramount to me (and still are, by the way). And while my parents divorced when I was just a few years old, I did see my grandparents' marriage as my guidepost. Their marriage wasn't by any means the lovey-dovey romance you see between some older couples, but you could tell they loved each other deeply. They had been through so much together, at such young ages. My grandmother was only eighteen years old when she and my grandfather married. He, on the other hand, was ten years older. They were both Jewish and were both from Austria. When you are eighteen and twenty-eight years old, fleeing your homeland as newlyweds to live in hiding in a foreign country, then arriving in a new land, leaving everything and everyone you know behind because of Hitler's persecution . . . it must feel

BEYOND overwhelming. As many times as I have thought about their experience, I still can't even fathom the depth of it all. I don't know how they did it, but I guess you figure it out when you are given no other choice and your lives are at stake. My grandparents were nothing short of incredible, and when you start your new life together in the way that they were forced to, you create a history together that is relatively unshakable. That was the marriage I saw. Not romance and roses, but somehow getting through it all—the good, the bad, and the ugly—together. For better and for worse.

In my mind and heart, this portrait of a rock-solid marriage was supposed to translate into my own life. But the honest truth is that I already had one failed marriage under my belt. I had married my college sweetheart, and while we shared some amazing times, it was a girlfriend-boyfriend relationship that never should have become more. My first husband was a wonderful guy who was kind, hardworking, and loved his family, but as we grew from college kids into graduated adults, we both began to realize that we simply didn't have that much in common. We were married for three years, made some wonderful memories, and then had the world's most amicable divorce. Yes, it hurt both of our hearts, yet no harsh words were ever spoken, no nastiness or bitterness. Truly just best wishes to two great people that discovered they just didn't have enough glue in common to keep them together. The friendship felt perfect, but the marriage felt forced.

From the time my first marriage ended to the time I met and began dating Mike, I focused my time and energy on my work and my relationships with my family and friends. I was doing well in my advertising sales career and loved the people I met and the flexibility I was able to have with my schedule. I didn't date; I just kept my head down and worked my tail off.

Then I met Mike. We dated for four years before getting married, and this time, I really felt like I had found the one. Was he perfect? No. But I loved his magnetic personality. His presence always made people feel invited in to let loose and have a good time. His charm was endearing, and his lofty goals and ideas were intriguing. He rarely got upset. The few times I saw it, however, his anger was like a volcano erupting. It didn't happen much, and we all have those less-than-stellar moments, so . . .

Mike proposed to me at one of our favorite resorts in Scottsdale. He arranged a small surprise get-together of our closest family to congratulate us on our engagement after he popped the question, and had even packed an overnight bag for me so we could stay at the resort for the weekend. We had so many wonderful times together in those early days when it was just us. We both loved to travel abroad, loved holidays, and loved our amazing friends—his, mine, and ours. We were both obsessed with personal development, and it was really Mike who opened my eyes to so many gifted thought leaders in the personal-development space. We would travel all over the country, learning from some of the brightest minds in entrepreneurship and leadership and spending hours talking about all that we learned and would incorporate into our business and our lives. Now, we did have lots of rocky times, too, when we were starting and expanding our business. There would be anger about finances and how he wanted things to grow faster, but I just chalked that up to the growing pains of any small business. It was part of the journey. As those early years ticked by, the decision to start a family was easy. We knew that we both wanted children and agreed that two or three would be ideal. And as our daughters entered the world, my heart was doubly filled.

But being parents to two very young children, growing a start-up business together, building a home, and finding time for everything else in life was a lot. And somehow the foundation that I thought was so sturdy was crumbling beneath me.

We had settled into our rental home while our new house was being built. The girls had adapted well, and little Alex would spend her days "cooking" in her pink play kitchen or whipping around the living room on her little yellow plasma car. (If you don't know what these things are, it's worth the Google search ... hours and hours of entertainment!) From the time she was an infant, Alex had a special intensity and a "knowing" about her. When people saw her when we were out and about, they would always comment with the exact same words: "My goodness, your baby is SO ALERT!" She was always looking everywhere, at everything. And she had a kind of nurturing quality to her, taking care of everyone around her, whether it was her baby sister or her favorite baby doll, "Zoogie." I could see this loving characteristic within her, but I hadn't truly experienced her sensitivity and sense of "knowing" until I needed it myself.

It was October 15th, 2008. It was now fall in Arizona, which means absolutely nothing because October in Arizona is hotter than most people's summers. The daytime temperatures were still over one hundred degrees, and we were certainly "over" the heat and ready for it to cool down, which typically happens right around Halloween. We were ready for our version of autumn and all the fun that fall brings. I couldn't wait to take the girls to the pumpkin patch together this year, now that Iliana could walk and explore all the fun firsthand.

It had been a busy day spent together, the girls and me. Mike was working on his computer quite a bit more these days. He used to join us for playtime at the park and for lunch, seeing as we worked from our home and had the flexibility to do so. But those days were seeming fewer and further apart ever since the move. He hadn't unpacked a single box—not one. And I really did my best to ignore it and be understanding of the hours he was putting in on the computer to grow our business. But something was just not feeling right. There was that shift that I had felt.

And I couldn't help but think back to that day—the grip on my arms and that damn flick to my neck—and all the raised voices and arguments in between.

No, it wasn't an isolated incident. It was a pattern. And it was getting both more frequent and more intense. So much of his frustration was now pointed at me. So much snapping and yelling and crazed looks of anger that often resulted in more of those arm and wrist grabs.

This wasn't the man I married. He was becoming . . . mean.

Yet, my attention would always, and easily, get pulled back to my two babies that needed my energy and attention. I would push Mike's behavior as far out of my mind as possible.

On this particular warm October day, the girls and I had gone to the park with some of my new mommy friends and their kiddos. I felt so lucky to have met these women, and even back then I knew our friendship was something special. It had been a long day of playing and the girls were tired, so it was time for an early dinner and bath before heading off to dreamland.

Mike was typing away on his laptop as I got the girls all bathed and smelling of that beautiful, clean baby smell. There was nothing I loved more than getting them all squeaky clean and doing our sweet little bedtime routine. We would snuggle up and read books and then I would put Iliana to sleep; she was the easiest when it came to naptime and bedtime—the complete opposite of her hyperalert big sister. Alex's bedtime routine was much more of a process. Alex and I would read and then would go through a series of little sing-along books that she loved. She would choose which ones she wanted and, ultimately, would pick the same ones night after night. Alex loved to have me read books that she was familiar with in anticipation of the funny ending or the surprise "peekaboo" element that would appear.

I cherished these priceless moments with each of my darling girls. My heart was so filled with love for these two little angel babies of mine. Each evening as we did our little nighttime ritual, I would think to myself how I truly was the luckiest girl in the world.

I finally got Alex to settle herself down and drift off to sleep. There was always the question of whether she would STAY asleep, but for tonight, it seemed like we were in the clear. I was definitely exhausted after another long day of running around with the girls, park time, and getting work done at home and for the business, so I was excited to just relax for a bit now that the babies were off to dreamland.

I walked into the kitchen, and as I peered around the corner, I saw Mike still at his computer, working away. Just as I was walking toward him, his phone made a buzzing sound, alerting him of a new message. The phone was plugged into an outlet in the kitchen, charging away from him and his laptop in the living room. I was just a few feet away, so I grabbed his phone and began to walk it over to him. As I did so, I happened to look down and caught a glimpse of the screen . . . and there it was.

"I love you, baby. I can't wait to be with you."

What.

The.

Fuck.

I read it again: "I love you, baby. I can't wait to be with you."

I was in shock. My head began to spin. My heart was racing. *Breathe, Jodi . . . breathe. Just breathe . . .*

I read it again. This was a dream. This was a nightmare. *This couldn't be happening.* My heart began to beat faster and faster. I felt sick.

I turned around and walked toward him, my arm outstretched.

"What ... what ..." The words were stuck. I couldn't speak. Or think.

"What IS this?!?" I blurted out.

It was like everything suddenly went blank. I don't remember the exact verbal exchange from that point forward. I remember him talking. And getting angry. I remember confusion: *How? When? Why?*

And then, *Who??*

It was all swirling in my head like a kaleidoscope from hell.

"Is this a joke? This can't be real!! What is going on??! WHAT IS GO-ING ON??!?"

I felt dizzy, weak, breathless, and found myself gasping for my next inhale. Complete and utter shock.

"We haven't even seen each other in person," he attempted to explain.

It was an old high school friend that he had reconnected with on Facebook. Ah, the tool that connects and disconnects worlds in a few quick clicks.

Suddenly, it all made sense. *That's why he's always on his computer. It's not for us, our business, our family. It was never for us. It's to get away from us and to get to her.*

I don't remember exactly what he said to me. He said words, I know that much. In fact, he *screamed* words. I don't remember them. I remember the shock. I remember blanking out. Whatever he said or yelled wasn't loud enough for me to hear over the screaming confusion and disbelief that barked in my head and pounded throughout my body.

Tears were flowing. Pouring. I was so mad. And I was so sad. And I was so damn *confused.*

After more words, more tears, and more yelling, there were even more unanswered questions ...

Why? How *could* he? What about his family? What about ... US?

It was a whirlwind of emotion. And then, the emotion just stopped, because suddenly he wasn't there anymore. After hours of tears and words and anger, we both collapsed—he on the couch with his laptop, me curled up alone in our bed. At the crack of dawn the next morning, he packed up a few of his things in a small suitcase, picked up his fully charged phone, and walked out the door. He left. He left for California, for a business meeting, where she also lived. He drove off . . . and left us.

And he left "us."

Confusion, peppered with anger. And so many tears. I ached. My heart, my soul. I had been so naive. I truly believed that we were his world. But everything was a lie. *This* had been going on for months. Maybe longer.

In the following hours, I felt riddled with pain. I was numb, yet doing all that I could to remind myself to stay strong and positive for my girls. They would see and feel it all, and I knew I had to shield their little hearts from the worst of it. I wanted them to feel safe, and to know, above all else, that they were loved and would always be protected. I would keep my voice soft and comforting and assure them how much Mommy and Daddy loved them. As difficult as it was, I would bring up Daddy in our bedtime conversations to make sure that they knew, somewhere deep in their little souls, that no matter what, none of this was their fault. I had studied communication and family studies for far too many years in college to not put all those skills to use when the rubber met the road . . . literally and figuratively.

The next morning, Alex ran into my room as I sat gazing out my bedroom window wondering what all this meant and what our future would look like. Unsurprisingly, I hadn't slept much. She came up to me and asked me a question I had no answer to:

"Where's Daddy?"

Beats the hell out of me, I thought to myself. Even though I knew he was with *her*, and not his daughters or his wife. Instead of holding on to the pain still pounding inside, I scooped Alex up and snuggled her.

"Daddy isn't here right now," I said quietly. "He's in California. But do you know what? Your daddy loves you sooooo much."

The words fell out . . . without effort. It was true. Their daddy did love them. He simply loved himself more.

During the next four days, I didn't hear a word from him. Not. One. Word.

But nothing in our little world changed. We had breakfast time and watched *Curious George, Little Einsteins,* and *The Wiggles,* just like we always did. We went to the park and swung on the swings. We did bath time and our little bedtime routines. Nothing changed, while everything was changing.

And then, just as I thought the silence would stay forever, the phone rang.

"I just wanted to let you know I'm fine."

"You're fine?" I said. "YOU'RE FINE???!!"

My blood was boiling.

"Do you have any idea how hard this has all been on me?" he responded.

Hard on YOU? I thought. *What about your girls? Have you thought about what they might be thinking or feeling right now? What about your wife? What about all of us you decided to leave in your wake?*

After that "trip" to California, he came back to Arizona and stayed at his mother's home. Over the next few days and weeks, we did the things we were supposed to do. We went to counseling. We talked. We took the steps.

To no avail.

I quickly saw there was no hope of reconciliation. Not just because he thought he had fallen in love with this high school friend. That wasn't the reason.

It was me.

I was finally done. I knew I deserved more, and better. And any man that can walk out on his wife and children, and be such a coward through it all . . . Well, that wasn't a man at all. And certainly not the one for me.

The days turned into weeks. Mike left for days on end to visit her in California. And while I was doing a lot of thinking, and a lot of soul-searching, I knew that life as I knew it was over forever. Our business would be gone. And I would inherit half of the business debt. The dream home and all that money we had put down on it would be gone too. I couldn't finish building it or afford it without an income anymore.

I forced myself to eat. The weight was falling off, and it was falling off fast. Twenty-one pounds in a matter of weeks. I was so thin and looked so frail. But something inside me was changing. I knew I was getting stronger, even though my body didn't show it. I was feeling my power growing inside of me—some kind of inner resolve to come out of this with no trace of being a victim. After all, my grandparents and my father collectively taught me that resilience was a part of our nature, a part of who we are. I wasn't about to let this hand simply be dealt to me and crumble because of it. No. I was coming out of this as a WARRIOR. I had this. WE had this. Nothing was gonna mess with me and these girls. I began to realize, in those low lows, that I was actually made for this moment. I would rise, and I would rise stronger than ever.

It was shortly after Mike had left us that his mother, Rose, came over to the house. She, too, was in utter disbelief. We had become her family, and she was devastated. She sat on the couch and I sat cross-legged on the floor while Iliana napped and Alex played in her pink toy kitchen.

"What happened to him, Jodi? Why would he DO this? This is not my son!" she said. She was doing all she could to fight back the tears but her voice quivered.

I remained calm, present, intact. I had to, for my girls. They needed to see and feel the strength within me. And in that moment, I decided: I had a new title.

Role model.

Yup—I was not only going to get through this, but these little girls and I were going to throw on our marching boots and figure this out together. I didn't know where we were headed, but I trusted that I would get us there one way or another. Because I wasn't just their mom anymore. I was now hyperfocused on being their role model, and it was up to me to show them that we *can* get through hard things. Really hard things. That we are going to get knocked to our knees. And when we feel like we just can't get up, we figure out a way to do exactly that.

While Alex was playing in her kitchen with her back facing us, I did my best to calmly explain to Rose that I didn't see the red flags from Mike. It simply happened right under my nose. Rose was beyond heartbroken.

"You all are my family. He is ripping us all apart . . . Jodi why would he do this? Was there something else?" she asked.

My biggest concern in that moment was to watch my tone and my energy, because I didn't want Alex to see me crying or feel me getting upset. I was doing all I could to comfort Rose and remain strong for my little girl. I continued, in an even-keeled voice, to explain to Rose that there truly wasn't anything else going on between Mike and me.

He just had become engrossed in his laptop and had been getting more and more short-tempered with me and the kids. In hindsight, he had really distanced himself from us a lot over the past several months.

Of course, it takes two to tango, and I knew that I was far from perfect. And perhaps my focus on the girls is what led us here, and led him to her and away from us. Perhaps I wasn't being as attentive to him or listening as actively as I could have. Either way, this was our current situation and it was time to take those first steps and guide these girls forward.

And yet, as I was saying all of this as calmly as possible to Rose, I looked over at my little Alex, who had decided to leave her kitchen and march right over to the bathroom. She stepped up on her little white step stool and reached over to the tissue box, pulled out a tissue, and promptly walked it over to me. As she handed me the tissue, she didn't say a word, but simply sat down in my lap and nuzzled her sweet little head up against my chest.

While I wasn't crying on the outside, somehow my little Alex could see the invisible tears within. She knew what I needed when I didn't even know. She felt it without even knowing what she was feeling. She just . . . knew. And in a way, even though I decided I was going to be a role model to my little girls, in that moment, they were role models to me, too.

Dear U,

On that painful October evening in 2008, I didn't realize how my life would forever change in the blink of an eye, or in this case, the reading of a text message. What I did come to realize, quickly though, was that I had years' worth of tools at my fingertips for this very moment—for these painful hours, and the days and years ahead.

I have been a student of personal development since my early twenties and here's what I MUST convey to U, as I feel it is both my duty and moral obligation: **INVEST IN U!!!**

Because here's the deal—all of those seminars I attended, books I read, courses I took, speakers I listened to, papers I wrote, assessments I completed, podcasts I listened to, thought leaders I spoke with ... EACH AND EVERY ONE of them taught me something to keep me grounded when challenges come. Because challenges will always come. And what I didn't know, back on that fateful day in October, was how incredibly well equipped I was to handle the future that lay ahead of me. Was it because I was somehow special or gifted? Not even a little bit—it was simply because I chose to continually challenge and work on myself by investing in personal development.

This, dear reader, is the ultimate takeaway. **U are your greatest asset**, and whatever knowledge and life experiences U acquire on this great journey called life, no one can take away from U. Because even though the path of life will have its twists and turns, the great news is that with every setback, heartache, and turn of events, U will grow stronger and wiser...

IF ...

U learn how to reframe setbacks as lessons learned. There is an opportunity in every challenge. There is a blessing in every heartache. Even the MOST difficult and painful moment in life holds some kind of lesson to be learned; U just need to seek it.

U build that muscle of self-confidence. The more U exercise it, the more it grows. Like any other muscle, U must keep pushing and challenging yourself so that U expand well beyond where U are today and become the person U are meant to be. Why live a life less than what U are capable of living?

U discover how to become self-aware. This means that when U recognize your own role in these challenges, U take ownership and accountability for your actions and behaviors. U are the sum of all of your thoughts and actions, so choose the good ones. And when U mess up (and U will, because U are a freaking human being and that's what we do), find the lesson to be learned, remember it, learn from it, own it, and don't let it happen again.

Dear reader, I can't say this loud enough, **BOLD** enough, in ALL CAPS enough:

Let reading this, right now, be the deciding moment for U.

DO IT! Say YES! Invest in U and your future. Pay the money, carve out the time. If any course or adventure or growth opportunity speaks to U in some way, in any way, say YES! And although U may not see or realize the benefit immediately, there will come a day when U are faced with a challenge greater than U could have ever imagined, and the tools will be there because **U chose to sharpen them, strengthen your confidence, and prepare yourself for whatever battle lies ahead.**

Life isn't always easy, but I believe in U. And now, it's time for U to believe in U.

With love and gratitude,

CHAPTER THREE

When Les Is More

To each there comes in their lifetime a special moment when they are figuratively tapped on the shoulder and offered the chance to do a very special thing, unique to them and fitted to their talents. What a tragedy if that moment finds them unprepared or unqualified for that which could have been their finest hour.
—Winston Churchill—

It was a typical spring evening in Arizona, except nothing about it was typical at all. The house was empty, so very cold. There were no little voices, no pitter-patter of tiny feet. No "Mommy! Mommy! Look what I did!" being heard from across the house. It was unfamiliar, yet it was quickly becoming all too familiar, and I didn't like anything about it.

This was one of the first evenings I spent alone without my daughters since Mike left us back in October of the year prior. They had been gone for maybe a day or so to see him, but I was just settling into this unfamiliar "new normal" and the eerie silence was deafening. I am not much of a TV watcher, but I decided I needed to do something to quiet the quiet, so I turned the TV on in the family room, which, ironically and sadly, no longer had a family in it.

The TV had been left on channel 8, our local PBS station. At that time, my oldest daughter, Alexandra, who was three years old, LOVED *Curious George*. She would laugh out loud and roll around giggling as she watched all of the silly adventures "Georgie" and the Man with the Yellow Hat would go on.

Simply turning on the TV to see what channel had been left on was another sting in my heart reminding me of how much I missed my two babies and how painful this journey was going to be. I hardly paid attention to what was on; I was simply looking for some sound—some life—to fill the loneliness that hung in the air with the heaviness, yet weightlessness, of a tattered shroud.

I walked back to the kitchen to finish making myself a bite to eat. I don't recall what was for dinner that night, but it typically consisted of just enough nutrition to keep me upright and functioning. I was losing weight at a rampant rate due to all the stress, so I would force myself to eat at least little bits throughout the day to keep up my energy and strength. And there were always dark chocolate M&M's for "dessert." ALWAYS. And lots of them. *Mommy's happy pills,* I would think to myself! Hey, it seemed like a better solution than any other vice I could have turned to.

As I finished making my dinner, I heard a familiar voice come from the family room that took me by surprise. As I stepped closer to the family room, I realized this was the public television telethon season, and the voices I was hearing were the announcers looking for donors to "light up those phones" so we could speak with one of the many "operators that are standing by" to help in supporting local public television.

But out of all those voices, there was one voice that I knew very well. One voice I had heard dozens of times in my car, in my home . . . the voice of none other than the magnificent Les Brown.

In my pursuit of and passion for personal success and achievement, and throughout my exhaustive clamoring for more and more wisdom, I had figuratively fallen in love with Les Brown, a motivational speaker and legendary thought leader. I loved his simple, yet rich storytelling ability and the vulnerability with which he shared his life experiences. He would talk about how nothing is impossible with enough conviction and belief, but you have to *want* it. You have to be HUNGRY for it. Oh, how I loved his excitement and enthusiasm for living a big, bold, purpose-filled life. He embodied that passion and fire that I recognized was also within me, that was yearning to break out and break free. His work, and thus his voice, from all of the audio recordings I listened to replaced that shroud and felt like a cozy, warm blanket helping to fill the cold and lonely room where my family used to laugh and play together.

As I turned the corner and looked at the TV, I saw him there on the screen—that big bright smile, that powerful and commanding voice, and that endearing, high-pitched chuckle. Turns out, Les Brown was in the PBS studios to promote a fundraiser he was doing to support public television. He explained that in just a few days, he was coming to Phoenix to host a live personal-development event at the PBS studios, and if you made a donation tonight . . .

I couldn't run to grab my wallet fast enough. I think my jog across the house became a full-blown sprint because I knew the value of this opportunity and I sure as hell wasn't going to miss it.

———

Now, let me back up.

Since the late 1990s, I had become a bit of a personal-development junkie. While I had been introduced to some of the theories and studies in college, it was oddly enough my soon-to-be-ex-husband that really introduced me to the multitude of thought leaders—such as my favorite Les Brown—that would forever shape my life and destiny.

But before I was ever married *or* divorced, I was simply a college student at Arizona State University, where I majored in communication with a minor in family studies. Prior to declaring my major, I thought I wanted to be a teacher. I love people and I thought working with children would be wonderful . . . until I realized that if I wanted children of my own one day, which I knew I did, that would be a LOT of time with kids and not much time with adults. I decided that ratio wouldn't work too well for me and that being a teacher ultimately wasn't the right path. Instead, I pursued communication as a major and fell in absolute love with my classes. Even the most difficult communication and rhetorical theory classes were engaging—so much so that I became a teacher's assistant for the course that practically every communication student detests! But I wasn't like every other student. I was all in . . . completely *engrossed.* I loved asking the big questions:

Why do we do what we do?

Why do we think and act in the ways we do?

And *It's all a choice?? I have that much power over my mindset and there are boatloads of communication tools and practices that can help in every area of life and business?*

Ooooh . . . I was loving this. Being a communication major gave me the people piece that I loved, the theory and *why* continuously wrangled my curiosity, and the demand for creative thinking allowed me to dream big. A perfect fit.

During college, I had a few different internships that allowed me to keep exploring this passion for people and human interaction. I worked in destination management and I worked at a couple of local radio stations as an intern. Although I enjoyed the companies and people I worked with, something was off. I felt uninspired. They were all just "jobs." The whole work schedule of punching a clock didn't appeal to me. I longed, even at a young age, to do work that *mattered* . . . something that felt exciting and created a lasting impact.

Now, I must admit, I have a *massive* work ethic. I work my tail off for anything and everything that I want, and if I am passionate about something, I am relentless. Believe me, I know that's not everyone's MO; however, I do believe that *everyone* craves that passion, that spark, that ability to feel a true sense of fulfillment. I have an insatiable drive to go after things and make them happen, and for some reason, nothing I was doing felt exciting or inspiring. That's what I sought and wondered about: What would light me on fire? What would be so interesting and exciting that I would want to wake up and do it each and every day?

As I graduated, I was hired on by a local radio station (I had made some great connections from my internships) and found my way into sales. But what the heck did I know about sales? And I was selling . . . "air"?! I was a little concerned that I might not be cut out for this. I pictured the cheesy image of the used car salesman in the brown polyester suit of the '70s, with the butter-yellow ruffled shirt and just enough chest hair popping out to make you want to gag. *Oh no, is this what is to become of me?? Am I going to be coerced into memorizing slick sales scripts and be summoned to drink coffee when I closed the deal?!* (Those of you old enough to know, know: "ABC! Always be closing! Coffee is for closers!") The thought of this picture made my stomach turn—this was *not* what I was looking for, but it was the only thing I could envision when I heard the word *salesperson*.

Yet, thankfully, once I stepped out of my comfort zone and into the world of sales, I realized none of this imagery that I had envisioned was real. No, it wasn't real at all.

I found out that sales was definitely a better fit for me and my personality than any of the work I had done up until that point. I was able to genuinely connect with people. I could ask about their hopes and dreams for their businesses and for their lives. I stood firm in my conviction that I was a resource, and if I genuinely could help them and be of benefit to them, terrific; if not, there were plenty of other business owners who needed this same kind of support. It was simply my mission to find those that needed me and help them. End of story.

I also knew that no matter what sales position I took, I would never have to be a salesy salesperson in order to succeed. That salesy vibe was inauthentic and I wanted to be *me*. I HAD to be me. I wanted to connect with people and help solve their challenges with them, help their businesses grow and be successful. For so many of them, this was their American dream, and to be a small part of them "winning" invigorated me. I realized sales was the avenue for me because it also gave me the freedom and flexibility to have more control over my schedule, something that I quickly realized was absolutely crucial for my existence. Freedom was an important value of mine that I recognized even in my early twenties.

From my stint in radio, I ended up finding my way into print advertising sales, direct mail sales in particular, and that's where things really took off. I got to work from home, set my own schedule, have a direct impact on small business owners' success and their livelihoods, and I could make as much money as I wanted, just by working hard! Sign. Me. UP!

Not only did I love it, I did very well at it. For years this was my path. I went from selling "air" to selling "junk mail," and I was thrilled. Life was good. As time went on and years progressed, the owners of that company changed direction (and the compensation plan) because we were making too much money in their opinion. That's around the time I met my husband, and voilà . . . a new idea was presented.

Entrepreneurship.

Wow. The idea was both scary and invigorating, all at once.

I should probably say that I come from a family of entrepreneurs. My father is an artist and an interior designer and always worked for himself. My grandparents were involved in putting together real estate and land deals, where they opened and operated homes for the elderly. And while I grew up around entrepreneurship, I never consciously looked at it as a viable option for me. It wasn't that I didn't think it would be a good fit for me—I simply never thought about it.

When I met this magnetic man, Mike, at an Oktoberfest party—

someone who was full of fun and energy and who set his own schedule and was his own boss—well, I was intrigued. His personality was charming, and we instantly connected. And as our romantic relationship grew, and as time rolled on, we worked together day in and day out to build our business. We both loved working with people and became energized by creativity and big thinking, so things naturally began to blossom. The business we built together was in the health and wellness industry and we were able to help a lot of people through what we did. It was exciting, and very challenging, but I loved being my own boss and setting my own schedule.

That's when I realized ... THIS was my path! Entrepreneurship! I never had toyed with this idea prior to meeting Mike, but once I got a taste of it, I was hooked and there would be no going back. The rest of my time on this earth would be spent building my own business. I simply knew it.

At the same time we were working on this business, I was reading more books and attending more lectures and seminars than I had in all my years of college. I was a voracious learner. *How do the most successful entrepreneurs do it? What do they do each day and, most importantly, how do they think?* My hunger for this knowledge grew like giant kelp on the ocean floor. What I learned about entrepreneurship and having an empowered mindset was so magnificent, so powerful! And we were using these tools of knowledge every day. We were building our dream!

Until that dream shattered before my very eyes, on the small screen of an iPhone, in the simple words of a text message.

But that's another story ... one you already know ...

––––

The day came. I was finally going to be seated in a huge auditorium with thousands of other adoring fans to hear one of the greats, one of the legends, Les Brown. My girls were with their dad, so I knew they were being cared for, and I could focus all my energy on this big day. I could hardly contain my excitement! I decided to wear a favorite sharp-white jacket. You know, dressing for an occasion like this is no small feat—a girl has to look and feel her best. I paired the white jacket with some crisp black pants and a fun, yet smart, black heel. Bam! Here we go! Time to drive over to downtown Phoenix to learn from the best.

As I pulled into the parking structure, I wondered why it seemed so easy to park. No attendants to direct traffic. No cones marking a path. Once parked, I turned off my engine and hightailed it into the building. I must have timed my arrival just perfectly and avoided the crowds and traffic . . . I certainly was there plenty early. Forty minutes, at least.

Entering the building, I asked the gentleman at the front desk where the event for Les Brown was located. As he shuffled through the paperwork on his clipboard, I peeked around and realized no one was around me. *Where WAS everyone? Was I in the right place?* I began to doubt myself, but then the kind man at the desk showed me to the elevator and directed me where to go. Off I went, no questions asked!

When I walked into the room, I quickly became confused. There were about eight tables draped in simple white linens, with white plastic folding chairs huddled together around the back side of each table to create a good view of the stage. And then there was a stage . . . or perhaps it would better be described as a riser. A small riser, at that, with a basic brown podium perched to the side. There was camera equipment and hundreds of wires and cables strewn throughout the room.

The entire set up felt like we were in some strange "behind the scenes" staging area, where cameramen and grips would hang out between takes, prepping for their next scene. It all seemed so out of sorts, thrown together like some lackluster afterthought of an idea that some producer had in a late-night dream. I remained confused. *Where are the crowds of people? Where are the red velvet stanchions keeping the hoards of people at bay and entering in an organized fashion?* All the while, I sat in my little white plastic folding chair directly in front of the center of that riser, alone in this empty space, wondering.

It was now thirty minutes to "showtime" and an elderly couple shuffled in and found their way to a table not too far from me. I looked around, wondering yet again if I was in the right place, when I overheard another gentleman asking that same question. He was reassured that yes, this was where Les Brown was going to be speaking in roughly thirty minutes from now. I remained confused, and yet insanely excited. This man filled the Georgia Dome with over thirty thousand people! Was I actually going to see him speak today, and was it truly going to be in this bizarre makeshift storage space with seating for MAYBE fifty people?!

The time ticked away as the room slowly began to fill while my heart began to race and my excitement began to bubble over. It was almost time, and then . . .

There he was. Mr. Leslie Calvin Brown. I saw him gaze out at the tiny crowd as he hopped up the single step of the riser to approach the podium. He looked . . . different. Disappointed, maybe? His eyes were squinted and had an intensity to them that I hadn't expected, and there was a furrow in his brow.

Yet, he dove right in. He began sharing the story of how his life began in Liberty City, Florida. How he and his twin brother were born on the cold floor of a run-down home. How he was labeled "educationally retarded" as a child and told he wouldn't amount to much. And he shared about his triumphs. How he did whatever it took to follow his desire to become a DJ, and how he kept on learning and growing and stepping into each new chapter of his life without letting anything or anyone stop him. I hung on every word. If someone were to claim that I didn't blink that entire morning, I would believe them.

And then, he stopped speaking. He decided to take a short intermission of sorts and hopped off the front of the riser.

And as I watched his every move, I realized he was walking straight toward me.

I was no more than twenty feet away as he began marching toward me with a few confident steps. The other two people at my table had meandered off already as I looked around wondering if anyone else was seeing what I was seeing. I bounced up off my chair as it appeared that he was walking up to . . . me! Was I in a dream??

The next thing I knew he reached out his hand and introduced himself to me. "Hi, I'm Les," he said to me.

Ummm, duh . . . yeah, I know! I have been a raving fan of yours for years and am hardly able to hold myself together in this moment, I thought to myself.

"Hi . . . hi . . . I'm Jodi," I paused and then quickly stuttered, "Jodi Low."

It was the first time I said my maiden name out loud, after so many years of not speaking it while I was happily married.

"So Jodi, what's your story?" he inquired.

My brain went into overdrive. My story? *Umm, my husband just walked out on my kids and me, I have about $40,000 in business debt, and*

I have no clue where I am going to live because the dream home we were building ain't happenin' anymore . . .

"My story?" I said. "Well, I have been a fan of yours for so many years and have read and listened to almost all of your work . . ."

Words were spilling out. Were they even making sense? *Holy shit,* I thought, *I am talking to Les Brown!*

"No, I mean, what's your story? What do you do?" he asked.

Well, currently I do my best to digest food. Then I do my best to not break down in tears in front of my children while comforting them and telling them how much their daddy, who walked out on them, adores them.

"Well, I am a coach . . . and a speaker . . ." I said, as I felt an immediate rush of warmth flood my face.

Oh . . . my . . . God. Did I just claim my new role out loud?

"Well, Coach Jodi . . ." he said with a huge grin, as he placed his hand on my shoulder, "You, my dear, have something I can't teach. Here's my card. Please give me a call tonight so we can talk."

He handed me his business card and quickly exited the room. I stood there, figuring out how to best pick my jaw up off the ground. Did I just speak directly to Les Brown? Did he just ask me to call him on his mobile phone?

More importantly, did I just introduce myself as Jodi LOW, a coach and speaker??? Who the hell is Jodi Low the coach and speaker? I was just in the midst of completing my master's certification in coaching and hadn't completed all of my hundreds of hours of facilitation yet. And a speaker? What the heck kind of a speaker was I? Sure, I had done training and development and had spoken in front of groups as Mike and I had built our former businesses together, but "A SPEAKER"? That seemed like a pretty bold title to proclaim to a man who had built his career doing exactly that.

As the rest of the morning progressed, I was in a haze, half mesmerized by the way Mr. Brown crafted his stories and lessons and half in awe of the fact that he had walked up to me, ME, the newly dubbed "single mom looking to figure her life and future out," wanting to connect. This must be a dream. And I certainly did not want to wake up.

As he wrapped up his incredible morning of insight and wisdom, he shared the emotion that I had read on his face when he first approached the stage. He explained that throughout his career he had spoken to sold-out stadiums filled with people hungry to learn from his words and his experiences. The disappointment I read upon his face was exactly that. He couldn't believe that when given the opportunity to make a small donation to support the arts and public television, only roughly fifty people in Phoenix took advantage of the opportunity. He wasn't sad for himself; it was obvious he was only sad for those that didn't understand the value in what they were missing.

As he graciously thanked the audience for saying yes to the opportunity and for being there, I, too, couldn't believe what a gift so many people never came to open that morning. I paused to consider this, and how very true the idea of missed opportunities is and the impact we have in our lives with each decision we make. Yet as I confidently approached the stage that morning, I didn't stop to second-guess myself. I boldly approached Mr. Brown, thanked him again for making the time to come meet me, and asked to have a photo taken of us on that stage.

That day, Mr. Les Brown did so much more than just say hello to me. In that moment, he planted a seed of belief in me. He allowed ME to begin to believe in me again, to step into my next level of greatness. He allowed me to ask myself, "Who am I NOT to be a powerful coach and speaker?" That empty and lonely void inside of me was being filled, as if I were a pitcher being filled with the sweetest homemade lemonade . . . the kind that makes you almost squeal in delight for its perfect harmony of sour and sweet. This was it. Jodi LOW was coming back bigger and better than ever.

A week or so passed, and during that time I not only used Les Brown's business card and called him back, but when we spoke on the phone, he explained to me that he always keeps his eyes open for speakers he can work directly with. People who have that "it factor," as he described. People who are coachable and teachable and who desire to grow their skills and speak around the world. Not long after, I also had the opportunity to speak with his team about what it would be like to continue on this incredible journey. His team told me that I would be working alongside Mr. Brown and some other talented speakers to hone my craft, to learn from the best of the best, and to have the opportunity to travel the country with them as one of his speakers, helping to open his talks and share the stage with him around the United States.

Wow!

The true "opportunity of a lifetime" that I had always heard about was staring me square in the face. The chance to work alongside, and learn directly from, one of the greats. A man that is a known legend in the field of personal development. Me and Les Brown; Les Brown and me.

And what exactly did he see in me? I asked myself. *What does he see that I don't see? We only spoke for a matter of minutes . . .*

Stop that thinking, Jodi . . . trust the process. This will all work out exactly as it should . . .

As the next week unfolded, I began to realize the true depth and breadth of this potential national-speaking circuit opportunity. The travel, the ability to empower others and share all of the wisdom I had absorbed over the years and years of personal-development study, and the travel. THE TRAVEL!! Shit . . . the travel. It sounded exciting, and even a bit glamorous. (Although, who are we kidding? I knew deep down that I was looking at a lot of Hampton Inns and Embassy Suites in my potential future. But that was okay.) This was an opportunity I could never have imagined, to speak in front of thousands, even tens or hundreds of thousands of people, and to work alongside one of the very best to help inspire others to see their greatness!!

How could I possibly do this??

I found myself in the deepest and strongest push/pull scenario I had ever faced: travel the country to build my career and leave my tiny babies with . . . who, exactly? My dad couldn't handle that on his own, plus he was busy working on designing commercial interiors for his own career. And my brother, well, considering he lived on the other side of the planet in Paris . . . Who would possibly be able to care for my little ones? How was I to be the mother I always wanted to be . . . to be there for all of the little moments, each and every one? And yet, how was I to forgo the dream of making a lasting impact on people across the nation as a coach and speaker? This was so difficult. A dream opportunity right in the palm of my hand. And two pairs of beautiful little hazel eyes looking up at me, belonging to two girls whose only want was to be with their mommy.

That same afternoon, I was at the grocery store with my girls, picking up some of our food for the week. I continually found myself at the local Fresh & Easy market because its brilliant concept allowed busy, chaotic, single, working parents like me the opportunity to pick up some healthy prepared meals that we could all share, while saving quite a bit of money, which was pretty darn scarce these days.

As I stood in line to check out, a toddler pulling at my leg and an infant squirming around in the cart, doing all she could to hoist herself out while I made every silly face and sound I could think of to distract her, my phone rang.

I looked down at the screen. An unknown number.

Hmmm, should I let it go to voicemail? I am sure it's someone wanting to talk to me about my car's extended warranty . . . nah. Just pick it up . . . you never know.

When I answered the call, I couldn't believe it. "Mr. Brown!" I said in a panic, surprised at the timing of it all. "Well . . . hello! How are you today, sir? So great to hear from you!" I spoke quickly and energetically, hoping I did my best to shush every dinging, buzzing, and whining sound around me. "Yes, I did speak with your team. And yes, I am beyond flattered. I would love to take you up on this incredible opportunity . . ."

As Mr. Brown asked the question, I knew it in my heart. I knew the answer days and days ago, but until now, this moment, I hadn't released myself and surrendered to it.

"Yet . . . I won't be able to," I said, exhaling a deep breath. "Mr. Brown, your belief in me and my potential is the greatest gift I have ever been given. Thank you . . . thank you so much. However, I am a single mother of two amazing young girls who desperately need some stability and who definitely need their mommy. And Mr. Brown, I need to be with them as much as they need to be with me."

Relief flooded me in that moment, knowing that I had said it aloud and owned it. And in the same moment I could feel the tears welling up in my eyes.

"Thank you for seeing something in me. I appreciate you more than you may ever fully know," I choked out through my tears with a shake in my voice.

He was so gracious and understanding on the other side of the conversation, and I . . .

I was just plain sad. However, as the words tumbled from my lips, I knew I was speaking my truth.

There was no choice. There was NO choice. My children were, and are, my lifeblood. There was absolutely no way, no how, that someone else was going to raise these girls. I refused to give up my children's life experiences, those precious and fleeting moments, the very essence of their childhood, in order to grow this career. I was heartbroken . . . truly and deeply.

Another loss of a dream . . .

Wait . . . No . . .

Just like that, I had an epiphany, right there in the checkout lane of Fresh & Easy. I was seeing this all wrong! This wasn't at all the closing of a dream; this was the birth of one!

I was given a gift . . . the best gift, in fact!

Because one of the most highly sought-after speakers on planet Earth had approached me—ME—and given me the literal and figurative tap on the shoulder. He believed in me. A stranger, a man who knew next to nothing about me, believed in ME! THAT was the gift.

Up until now, I didn't have the belief in myself or my abilities to be a coach, a speaker, and a mom. I had the drive, but drive without belief doesn't get you out of the cul-de-sac and onto the road of life. However, now I knew I could do this. I WOULD do this. And I was going to do it in my own way, on my own terms. I was going to build my company around MY life with my children. We would become a massive and powerful force for good. I was going to help create sustainable and life-changing programs and classes and offerings that I had yet to even become aware of or construct. And I didn't *need* to know how I was going to do it. The *how* was none of my business. All I needed to know was what I had just became acutely aware of . . .

I knew my *why*.

———

About a year and a half after that fateful day at the PBS studios, I had the privilege and opportunity to see Mr. Brown speak again. This time, I reminded him of who I was, and how disappointed I had been about not being able to work with him. Remembering me, he asked how things were going, and I told him about the building of this little dream of mine that I had begun to see slowly bloom before my eyes. I had graduated as a certified coach; I was coaching clients and doing complimentary speaking for numerous local corporate and charitable events. Whatever it took, I was doing it, and saying yes to every opportunity that came my way. My clients were referring others to me, and I had begun doing small group coaching and training, all while still being there for my girls to take them to school each morning and pick them up every afternoon.

In those dark early post-divorce days, when I was feeling empty and caught in the void, I wondered, "Can I really have it all?"

Damn straight I can . . . WE can. It really was possible. We were making it all possible, me and these little girls of mine. With passion as my fuel, and the conviction to be a role model for these girls and to show them that they, too, can be, do, and have anything they want in this world, the future was ours to create, and creating it was just what we were doing.

After telling him all of this, Les and I shared a laugh over the sheer joy of it, and of course we had another "photo op."

After all, I MUST capture those incredible "life moments" whenever I can.

———

I saw Mr. Brown speak many years later and in a much larger venue at an event in Phoenix. As he was the keynote speaker, I knew there would be no opportunity to speak with him face-to-face due to the sheer volume of people attending.

It had been seven years or so since we last spoke, and a lot had changed. I had changed. I wanted to let him know. Not about me and what I was doing, but about the enormous impact he had made on one woman's life, and, in turn, the lives of her two, now elementary-school-aged, girls.

So I wrote him a letter, explaining what he had done—the powerful impact of that tap on the shoulder so many years ago. I let him know it was that moment that gave me the belief in myself to go after the new dream I had been building only in my mind up until then. I let him know that he not only helped to shape me and my future but the future of my daughters. I let him know that because he rested his hand on my shoulder that morning, I had done it! I was doing it! My grocery store epiphany was a reality, all thanks to the belief of a stranger.

And to this day, that photo hangs on my office wall, a perfect reminder of the power of a stranger's words and the impact that one person can have on the life of another.

Dear U,

Life is filled with a multitude of beautiful lessons, or *gifts*, as I like to call them. Sometimes, these little gifts appear as fleeting moments, and if noticed and appreciated, they can teach us wisdom that will last a lifetime.

Whether these gifted moments appear in the form of a chance encounter, a meeting with someone who shines a light onto something U never noticed or saw before, or even a text message sent at just the right time, they are often opportunities that present themselves in an obscure place and time and have the power to shift the trajectory of your life, if paid attention to and acted upon.

When I met Les Brown that day—post-divorce and feeling empty and confused about the direction my life was headed in—I had no idea that one meeting would plant the seeds of confidence within me. That one single moment could hold up a mirror to my own gifts and show me that I could truly become a coach and a speaker, which would ultimately lead me to founding U & Improved. This moment with Les Brown instilled a new view of myself as a leader. It was a gift beyond measure.

My dear reader, to truly see yourself as a leader, U must:

Be aware of those gifted moments. Don't let them pass you by; instead, hold them close inside of you. Recognize them, dissect them, ask more questions for clarification, if necessary, and look for your own answers.

Once the seed of confidence is planted, it's your job to water it. Nurture it. Don't let it die. If you put in the time and effort to tend to this confidence, this belief within yourself, U will reap the benefits and truly blossom. It takes consistency and patience; however, small, actionable steps create a compounding effect over time, and it is out of consistency that positive new habits are formed and shift truly happens.

Share your gratitude. Take the time to reciprocate the kindness of this planted seed and let the person who shared their thoughts and insights with U know of the impact it has made upon U. Hearing how they have made a difference in your life and future is a beautiful gift that U now get to reciprocate.

And remember U, too, can give back when U are given the precious gift of a "belief moment," and U get to do that in the form of sharing brilliant experiences and moments that U notice in your interactions with others. The reality is that we all have someone who deserves to hear that we believe in them, that they have touched our lives in a meaningful way. So my question for U then is this: Who do U truly believe in? Who needs and deserves to hear from U about the brilliance U see within them?

Say it to them. Share it in words ... both written and verbalized. What a beautiful way to pay it forward.

With love and gratitude,

the
Communicator

———

CHAPTER FOUR

Castaway

Some people come into your life just to teach you how to let go.
—Author Unknown—

Remember when I mentioned being in my early twenties, selling "air" at the local radio station? Fresh out of college, I knew nothing about sales, but quickly realized I loved genuinely connecting with people. And the world of sales was a revolving door of connections to be made. One such connection happened with a woman named Marie. Because I was selling airtime, our paths crossed on more than one occasion. What I didn't know back then was just how much this meeting would change my life forever.

At the time, I was young and in my twenties, and ever ready to get things done. Marie was a little bit older than me and owned a media buying company with her husband, Greg. I didn't see Greg too often, but Marie and I would always manage to strike up a conversation when we would run into one another. As time went on, we got to spend more time together, expanding our relationship. Marie and I always seemed to have enjoyable conversations; she was engaging and had creative ideas to share about what she and Greg were up to, and I loved hearing about their latest business ventures.

One day, Marie called me out of the blue and asked me if I knew of anyone that would be interested in a work-from-home advertising sales position. I was a bit taken aback, as we rarely spoke on the phone. Marie explained that she and Greg decided to run with their booming entrepreneurial spirit and start a direct mail company targeting businesses in the valley. You know, the kind of "junk mail" ads that come in an envelope that you sift through directly over the trash can, perhaps siphoning out the one or two that grab your attention. But they wanted to do things differently by focusing on neighborhoods that would have the discretionary income to spend at local businesses and making sure to hone in on creating an exceptional customer experience.

And although I didn't know much about Marie and Greg personally, what I did know was that Marie and Greg were *sharp*. They knew how to get people excited and appeared to be very successful. Marie was always dressed to the nines with the most eye-catching handbags and the highest of perfectly pointed heels. She had an undeniable confidence to her walk and made heads turn upon entering a room. Greg, on the other hand, was just plain goofy. Although he had a silly laugh and made wild hand motions when he spoke, people were drawn to his quirky personality. While I believe most people felt deep down that it was Marie who was the driver behind the enterprise, opposites do attract, and there was something magnetic about the pair of them.

So, when Marie posed the question to me on the phone that afternoon, asking if I happened to know anyone interested in an opportunity like this, I immediately said, "That's something I would be REALLY interested in!"

Not long after that initial phone call, Marie and I met to discuss the position. I knew selling airtime wasn't my lifelong dream, and while I didn't know WHAT that lifelong dream was at the time, I did know that something that would give me more flexibility in my life sounded right up my alley. I had (and have) a massive work ethic, and with my love of autonomy and practicality, working from home on my own schedule made a ton of sense to me. I quickly knew this was the next stepping stone in my career, and I took the leap.

My career with Marie and Greg's direct mail company was incredible. I loved my clients, I loved meeting new people and helping to creatively grow their small businesses with them. I also loved the freedom and flexibility this independent contractor role provided. And unlimited income potential? Sign. Me. Up. Additionally, an unforeseen gift came with this career move: my friendship with Marie and Greg really began to blossom. At first, it was just a few of us on this tiny team, as Greg and Marie's business literally grew right out of their garage. This kind of small business thrived on entrepreneurial spirit and because we all worked so closely together, friendships were bound to form. Greg and I would go to meet clients together, and while he was awkward and silly, there was something endearing about him, and we would laugh nonstop throughout the day. On top of that, Marie was always inviting me to exciting events around town. It was such a fun career, working with exceptional people. I worked my tail off and as the company continued to grow, I became one of the top account executives in their small company. I was having the time of my life, and I couldn't imagine anything better.

Always seeking ways to incentivize us, Marie and Greg loved to create sales contests for fun vacation destinations, and part of the prize was that they would go on the trips as well. We traveled together, staying at some beautiful resorts throughout Southern Arizona, and took trips to gorgeous seaside destinations like Puerto Vallarta, Mexico. Marie and I would talk and sip a cocktail or two, lounging and reading by the pool, having an absolute ball. We became closer and closer, laughing for hours and sharing stories over amazing meals. She truly became like an older sister to me.

As the years moved on, the direct mail company grew, and Marie and Greg decided it was time for them to expand their business, so they started a local magazine, highlighting all of the "latest and greatest" in lifestyle, home, fashion, events, and more that were happening in the area. As the magazine became more and more successful, they asked if I would like to sell advertising for the magazine instead of working on the direct mail side of the business. But things were going so well with the direct mail; I adored my clients and loved what I was doing, so I politely declined.

Soon, the magazine became one of the hottest lifestyle publications in the state. Understandably, Marie and Greg began to devote more and more attention to that product. Things were still going very well with the direct mail company, but I could see the shift happening. They were falling in love with this new baby, the magazine, and their first baby, direct mail, was not where their time and energy were focused. I also began to see a shift between Marie and Greg. As an employee and dear friend of theirs, I could feel change happening around me in how they spoke to one another, with curt fragments of sentences and verbal "eye rolls" back and forth. Meanwhile, these tense exchanges were never apparent to the outsider. To the public, everything was incredible. However, the facade began to grow thicker and deeper, like fog rolling in to the San Francisco Bay on any given Northern California morning. On the inside, everything just felt different to me. And not a good different.

Never one for drama, I kept plugging along, dedicated to my position and still loving the work I was doing. It was at this same time that I met Mike, and as we began dating, I learned more from him about entrepreneurship and what it would be like to truly own my own business. I was intrigued, but I had such a good thing going with selling the direct mail. What I did seemed very close to being an entrepreneur in many ways, minus a lot of the headaches entrepreneurs face, such as accounting, hiring staff, and marketing. Yeah, those headaches didn't sound so great, so I kept working away.

With this job, I had the freedom, the uncapped income . . . It was *all* good.

Until one day . . .

Marie and Greg held a meeting in the sparkly new office they had recently opened to house the magazine staff. They asked the account executives to meet to discuss a few changes that would be taking place. We all gathered around the shiny conference room table, waiting to hear what was coming.

And here was my first big lesson in my career: don't get too comfortable, because the rules of the game can change at any time.

Marie shared all about the incredible success of the magazine and how thrilled they were at the sheer volume of clients who were loving their beautifully designed advertisements and the results of their marketing efforts. Greg chimed in about how the expansion of the magazine allowed them to target a more affluent demographic and create a luxury-brand magazine for the most elite clientele.

I knew this was incredible news for them. They were hardworking and deserved all the success they were creating. I was truly happy for them. However, I did realize that I was feeling a bit disappointed that there was little to no mention of the direct mail division of the company. I was definitely feeling like the old, loyal dog that sat quietly and patiently by the window waiting for her owners to come home, excited to see them and get some belly rubs. But all the owners' energy went to the cute, new little puppy. *But it was fine, really,* I told myself. *Why did it matter?* I convinced myself that it wasn't about the attention or accolades for our division of the company, as long as I could continue to do what I did: work with my clients and expand my clientele, work from home on my own schedule, and make limitless income. I was completely good with being the old dog. Call me Fido; that was A-OK for me.

And then, it happened.

Greg said the company needed to make some additional changes and those working in the direct mail side of the company were going to get a significant decrease in their pay. And I mean a MASSIVE slash in the commission structure. He also said that everyone would need to work from the office from now on.

. . . wait, what?!

I. Was. Pissed.

I was their second employee! I helped build this with them when they were working out of their garage! We had become dear friends who vacationed together and spent many nights out having dinner and drinks with one another . . . they were like my beautiful older sister and quirky older brother . . . *and THIS is how you are choosing to tell me this bit of news? No heads-up, no one-on-one conversation?* Strong relationships are based on trust and mutual respect, with honest conversations that honor both parties. This meeting in front of everyone didn't feel like that. This felt like an atomic bomb had just been dropped on my—and others'—livelihood. By not having an upfront, individual conversation, it felt like an easy way to sluff off this big change and bury it in the midst of all the great news about the company's overall success.

I kept the smile on my face as I walked out of the building that evening. I needed time to process this information. I needed time to simply sit with it.

Clearly, the rules had changed. And, in their defense, it was the game they created, so if they wanted to change HOW the game is played, that was their choice. I, however, didn't necessarily need to remain a player in the game.

As I pondered my future and my fate, I began to think about how things were now versus how they were before. I felt like I had been written off, lost in the shuffle of their rapid success. I felt like they had lost themselves along the way too, and had forgotten where they came from. The down-to-earth, fun-loving, "let's all do this together and crush it as a team" energy had faded. Meanwhile, it looked like Greg's quirky, outgoing personality had grown out of control, as he was partying like a rockstar. And to me, Marie simply seemed like she couldn't be bothered to talk and connect, having more important things to do. It was a gradual change, growing so slowly that I had missed it, or at least dismissed it, over the past few years. I hadn't seen it for what it truly was: a lot of success very quickly. I didn't like the energy of where things were headed with the company, and this wasn't the trajectory in which I wanted my career to go. It was time.

The following week, I went into the office for a meeting I had arranged with Marie and Greg. "We've had a lot of great times and done so many incredible things together. I have truly enjoyed my many years working with you both. However, after a lot of self-reflection, I recognize it's time for me to move on to my next opportunity," I said to them both.

"Seriously? You can't leave! You've been with us since the beginning!" Greg clamored.

I was happy he noticed . . . and remembered. He asked me if I wanted to come sell on the magazine side of the business, working with the most elite companies in the area and going to all of the luxury events.

But the glass slipper simply didn't fit me.

I loved my small business owners. I loved coming up with innovative offers and ideas to drive more business through their doors and seeing them excited by the wins they had along the way. I loved spending time chitchatting with them and acting as a bit of a guide and counselor to them when they just needed someone to talk to as the challenges of running a business became too much. I loved the underdog success stories and playing a part in making their American dream a reality. Those were my people: the ones who appreciated everything and were excited for their successes, even when they were seemingly small in the face of what the big, bold magazine clients were doing.

"I appreciate it, Greg . . . but it's time for me to move on," I said confidently. And as I walked out of the pristine office doors that day, I knew I would never turn back. This chapter was over.

Unknowingly nearing the end of my career in direct mail sales, I had grown more and more interested in what my boyfriend, Mike, was up to. I loved the products he was marketing and really loved the flexibility, income potential, and time freedom that went with it. This was my chance to start something new. This was my opportunity to have even more flexibility, independence, and income potential than I had had previously, and no one would slash my commission or make me work from an office.

After Mike and I talked about it and sincerely agreed it was the best move for me and for him, I pulled the trigger and joined him in building a business together, and that's where that ride began . . .

———

In those very early days after Mike left the girls and me, I began doing a lot of soul-searching. *Why was this happening? What was I supposed to learn from all of this? How would we move forward, and what was I going to do?*

The one question that I NEVER asked myself was "I wonder who is hiring?"

In hindsight, it's kind of comical to me now, but it truly never dawned on me to get a job. My question instead was "What am I going to *create?*"

I spent countless hours thinking, reading, and reflecting. I knew that whatever was next for me had to be something that mattered. Something I was passionate about. And it absolutely HAD to in some way serve people.

One morning I met with one of my friends, Eliza, a superbright woman who had traveled the world, had a couple of very successful careers, and was a true friend with a caring ear always ready to listen.

I explained over coffee that I knew I wanted to build something to help people. I knew I loved seeing people grow and succeed, seeing them truly blossom and believe in their dreams.

"Have you ever thought about being a coach?" Eliza asked.

"A coach? Like . . . for SPORTS??" I shockingly replied.

"Nooooo, not that kind of a coach. A life coach," she continued.

"A life coach? What's that?" I said, utterly confused.

"I think you would be so good at this, Jodi. You love helping people. You love personal development. There are degrees and certifications you can get to learn more and develop your own practice . . ."

The more she said, the more I found myself leaning in.

"You should really look into it—it would be perfect for you!" she said with excitement.

Hmm, a life coach.

Seemed sort of funny, given that, at the time, my life looked like a complete train wreck, to think of myself coaching others through their own trials and tribulations. But the seed of intrigue was planted that day, so I decided to investigate.

Now, if you know me, you know there is little in my life that I ever do "half-ass." I definitely subscribe to the "anything worth doing is worth doing right" school of thought, or from my perspective, "worth doing your best." So I read, read, and read some more about this career I had been totally unfamiliar with a week prior. I began to see and feel how this could really be a perfect fit for me. I could serve people, helping inspire them to take action on their goals and dreams through the clarity they would gain with coaching, all while creating a business around my top two priorities on the planet: those precious baby girls of mine. Check, check, and check-check. I was stoked. *I was going to do this.*

Through my research, I learned about a school just thirty minutes away that I could attend a couple of nights each week for the next eight months that would provide me with the knowledge, practical application, and hands-on hours needed to gain my master's certification in coaching.

Now, the logistics. How could I possibly be away two nights a week, learn and practice the curriculum, and complete the massive number of hours of actual coaching practice, all while raising a one- and three-year-old all on my own?

Enter my knight in shining armor. The man who has had my back and believed in me since the day I entered this world: my father.

My dad is the most unique father you could ever meet. He has been a fine artist and an interior designer his entire life and is one of the most giving people I've ever known. When I was telling him about this coaching idea, and the schooling that would go along with making it a reality, he jumped right into action, offering to watch the babies while I went back to school at night to make it happen. "But what about your art, your work?" I had asked, thinking about his own career, his own dreams. "For you, honey . . . anything. The girls and I can draw and play together," he quipped.

How lucky was I? Nervous about putting all of this on him for several nights each week for the next several months? Absolutely. But was it the best, and only, solution? Yup.

I didn't know how I would do it, or how WE would do it, but I knew WHY I was doing it. Those two little girls were the only motivation and focus I needed to jump in and figure it out. And with my dad having my back, I knew this would all work out. No question.

———

Those next ten months were a whirlwind. I was able to get all my little ducklings in their proverbial row and enroll in the coaching program at that top school I was looking at just a short drive away. The next program started in a few weeks, so I jumped in headfirst and didn't look back.

Simultaneously, I began to form my company name and brand. I knew that I wanted something memorable and unique that also embodied the type of work I planned to do. I am obsessive about language and words (a trait I adopted from my grandfather). A clever juxtaposition of language or a well-played pun can keep me engaged and laughing for hours, so I wanted that right name to come to me, and just as I was learning all about how to form a limited liability corporation with the Arizona Corporation Commission, the name arrived.

I knew that coaching is all about the client—*you*. And I knew that if the day or moment ever came that what I did became about me, then it would be time to chart a different course. I wanted a name with an anchor, something that would be a verbal and visual cue so that clients would always know that this work we did together was always, ALWAYS for, and about, them.

You . . . only better.

You . . . improved.

You and improved!

But it needed to be clever and memorable. It had the auditory appeal I was going for; now it needed the visual anchor . . .

U & Improved.

It's all about *U*. It's all for *U*.

Boom. This was really *happening*.

———

U & Improved started out as a coaching practice. I was dead set on helping people thrive, both personally and professionally, and I was determined to make an impact. It's what I loved and what I was excited to pursue. But I quickly realized I wanted more than this. I was inspired to help people in any way I could, and working with them individually was very rewarding, but it wasn't enough. If I wanted to create a larger reach, I needed a bigger platform. I just didn't have a clue yet what that platform could possibly be.

A few weeks later, my dad stopped by the house for a visit. We were lucky to live close to him, so the girls really had their grandpa in their lives more than many children. I felt so fortunate for that.

"You'll never guess who I ran into today!" he said excitedly as he walked into the kitchen.

"No idea. Who?" I said.

"I was at the grocery store and ran into Marie! We ended up talking for quite a while, and she was telling me how much she misses you and would love to reconnect with you," he continued.

"Oh wow, that's a name I haven't heard in a while! What's she up to these days . . . did she tell you?"

"Well, that's what was so interesting," he said. "She is becoming a coach, too, and she wanted to connect with you and see how you might be able to work together or help one another or . . . who knows what!" he said.

I thought about reconnecting and how nice it would be to see her after all these years, to catch up with each other, to hear what her ideas and plans were for becoming a coach, so I reached out and we decided to meet for coffee.

It was really wonderful seeing her after so many years. She seemed like she was in a really good place. She and Greg had divorced; she had sold her interest in the magazine to him; the direct mail company had been dissolved; and she was starting a new chapter in her life, much like me.

As we talked that day, she seemed really grounded and back to the Marie I had grown to love so many years ago. She was warm and endearing, smart as a whip and as sharp as ever. As we reminisced about the past and laughed about old, crazy memories, we also discussed our individual plans for the future.

And then, we started to brainstorm a bit.

And a little bit more.

We had worked really well together in those early days, and that synergy was showing up again for us now. We had always looked at things through a similar lens; looking now, we asked ourselves, *What if . . . ? What if we could create some kind of a place for people to grow and learn together? What if it was some kind of a school of some sort, where business owners could gain specific skills and knowledge? But what if we could take our backgrounds and life experiences and create specific courses, like at a traditional "school" or college, and allow business owners to dig even deeper into what they wanted from their lives and businesses?* Finally, the platform to reach so many people—just what I was looking for.

We were getting excited. Both of us have big picture, conceptual minds coupled with a tactical "how-to" approach, so as the ideas flew, and our pens hit paper, we started to gain more traction, and the seedling of an idea for educational courses was beginning to grow.

We continued to meet several times over those next few weeks, and it became more and more clear to us that we needed to really hone in on a specific niche of audience. While we loved the idea of helping anyone and everyone we could, we knew better than to be all things to all people.

Women. Women entrepreneurs, to be exact.

Both of us were women and entrepreneurs, so why not serve people whose trials and tribulations we understood better than anyone else?

And what would we call this learning space, this school for women entrepreneurs? The name had to be clever and intriguing and let women know it was a place where they would be supported and encouraged and feel like they belonged.

We sat in a coffee shop, sipping on lattes and tea, brainstorming for hours. We threw out ideas of what the company could be called, testing out clever turns of phrase. We massaged words and language, looking for that perfect fit.

And then it happened . . . the name hit us.

Girlfriend University.

A business school for female entrepreneurs and executives.

We sketched out logos and thought of locations where we could create this concept, and over the course of the next couple of months, it all began to crystallize and come together. As we stared down at the new logo we created, a silver collegiate *U* with *Girlfriend* written diagonally across it in hot-pink lipstick, we both felt a surge of adrenaline. Girlfriend U was here!

Then, we started to formulate content for our "classes," which were programs designed for women to grow, reflect, expand, and crush it in their personal lives and their business dreams. We also reached out to everyone we knew to let them know what we were up to and to invite them, their friends, and their colleagues to attend a complimentary class on us. Whether it was a class about business basics or the mindset of entrepreneurship, we had these ladies covered!

Things began to grow at Girlfriend University. Our gorgeous and over-the-top-girlie office welcomed new ladies every month, and word got out that "the Girlfriends" meant business . . . literally and figuratively! Marie and I were having a ton of fun building this together and seemed to have a great "divide and conquer" mentality. I created a lot of the content, while Marie handled all of the legal, bookkeeping, and technology-related pieces. We both filled classes and facilitated them, as we both found so much joy in doing so. That was by far our favorite part, watching those *a-ha* moments take place!

And then, something quite unexpected happened. Boyfriends arrived.

No, not men to date; rather, we were having more and more men ask if they, too, could attend our classes. Word was spreading, and apparently these gentlemen didn't want to be left out! We welcomed the guys into Girlfriend U, and as more and more men joined the classes, and more and more requests for corporate training came our way, we knew the inevitable must happen. The hot-pink, girly vibe needed to change. We needed to rebrand and rename this company. So Marie got the paperwork drafted, we had the hot-pink wall repainted red, and the next iteration, Amplify U, was launched!

Much like its predecessor, Amplify U would focus on personal and professional development, but for women AND men, and for teams and corporate clients that were looking for ways to "level up" their teams. As we expanded, so did our team. We knew we needed to expand our offerings and develop more rich and robust training, and I was fortunate enough to have met just the gentleman to help us with that expansion.

Dean was a seasoned trainer with years of experience in the

personal- and professional-development training world, and he was completely on board to help us create this expanded and expansive curriculum. We met at a leadership conference that I attended and quickly hit it off as friends and colleagues. Little did I know then the impact that meeting would have on my life and business. He had a brilliant mind for business and a big heart for helping people find their passion, and I knew that with his help and support, we could create some beautiful things together.

And we did just that. Amplify U began to expand its offerings to include two-and-a-half-day courses focusing on helping teams lead, not just manage, as well as helping individuals see their greatness and eliminate limiting beliefs. We created a class to help people stop working in silos and learn how to truly connect and build strong relationships based on trust and powerful communication. It was an exciting time and a scary time. Marie and I knew that we were headed in a beautiful new direction, yet we needed to introduce these immersion-based learning classes to people without anyone having experienced them. We needed real, honest feedback on how powerful these courses would truly be for others.

So we got on the phones and made calls and sent emails right away. We invited people to attend as our guest or perhaps at a nominal fee, and while we weren't making any money yet, we knew that once people experienced these classes firsthand, the profits would come. In those early days, we weren't focused on profits because we believed wholeheartedly in these classes and what they could do for people's lives and businesses. What mattered most was having people experience them, experience those *a-ha* moments, and realize the power of investing time and energy into growing themselves both as leaders and as human beings. Month after month, we hosted these classes and invited more and more people to attend. And they came. Sometimes, it was begrudgingly as a favor to us, but then, as they continued taking the class, the shift began to take place . . .

"This was the most powerful experience of my life!" we heard.

"If we had to choose between our wedding day and attending this course, we would choose this course every time, hands down. What this did for our marriage, and our business, is a gift that will last our entire lives," another couple shared.

"What you did with my team in two-and-a-half days would have taken us years to accomplish," one business owner said.

It was *working*. People were having those life and business transformations before our very eyes, and it was nothing short of magical.

As our courses continued to expand, so did our team. Dean had worked with a few other outstanding experiential-based learning trainers, and he offered them the opportunity to work with Amplify U and take their own new next step.

Expanding our team was the biggest gift. Each of these trainers brought it—heart, body, and soul—to every class they led. They were all in, and so was I. THIS was what I had dreamed of. This was what I had always envisioned. People began to describe their lives and businesses as "before Amplify U and after Amplify U"—it was THAT powerful and impactful of an experience. I was in tears and had goose bumps as each class graduated, pinching myself in disbelief that this was the work we GOT to do each day.

———

As time went on, and the business grew, I noticed that Marie became more absent from the office. She had meetings and appointments, and more meetings and more appointments—I did my best to keep my head down like a horse in the race of her life, with blinders securely fastened. I continued to share the powerful work we did with the world, while filling the seats in each of our upcoming classes. However, I was also becoming frustrated, as the workload was feeling less and less equitable. And a glimmer of that aloofness I had seen so many years ago in Marie had begun to resurface.

"So, I won't be in today. Lots of appointments out of the office," she said.

"Oh, okay . . . with whom?" I replied.

"Several clients are really interested in bringing what we do to their teams," she said, not missing a beat.

"Terrific . . . let me know how they go when you wrap up with them!" I said, hoping it was just my mind playing tricks on me. The details of these meetings and appointments were often never shared with me. I felt my trust waning.

I was feeling VERY alone in our business.

My fortieth birthday came all too quickly. Eliza and another dear friend surprised me in the morning with a beautifully set table with special birthday accoutrements, mimosas, and pastries. During the day, I celebrated with my girls and my dad, having a wonderful lunch together at one of my most favorite restaurants in Scottsdale. And in the evening, Marie picked me up in a shiny SUV with a driver, who chauffeured us to dinner while we sipped on champagne. Dinner turned out to be a huge surprise birthday party with all my loved ones and closest friends and colleagues. To top it off, the decorations included a life-size cutout of me, along with custom-designed champagne flutes with my picture on them. I was blown away. So much attention to every fun and funny detail, so much love . . . I was truly blessed to have such a wonderful group of dear friends. As the evening went on, my doubts with Marie seemed to disappear; she was a great business partner. Clearly, I had been feeling something that wasn't there, that wasn't true. Her absence was obviously just in my head. She really did care.

A few more weeks flew by. I came off my birthday high and jumped back into the busyness of building our business. The days were packed with phone calls and meetings, lunches and trainings. I loved all of it—the ability we had through these classes to truly transform lives.

But during those weeks, the absence of Marie was felt yet again. She would fly through the office doors, asking me to sign off on some paperwork or to drop something off, and then as quickly as she flew in, she flew out. Poof!

Another week of this, and another. It was starting to really grate on me. I didn't understand where she was and what she was doing, and any time I confronted her about it, I only received a curt response—something about a meeting with someone here and an opportunity there.

Once the frustration reached its peak, I resolved to set aside some time to talk about this face-to-face. I knew in my heart that an open and honest conversation about how we were both feeling would help alleviate the confusion and mistrust that was seeming to build between us. We arranged to get together a couple of days later, in the afternoon.

When that afternoon arrived, Marie asked me to meet her outside the office on a bench so we could talk. I felt like a child being called to the principal's office, with no idea what I had done. It simply felt . . . off.

There was a somberness to her voice as she glanced down at the concrete below us, her eyebrows raised. "So I've been wanting to talk to you too. It's been a while." Marie went on to tell me that she and a gentleman friend were becoming serious. He and another successful entrepreneur in town were expanding some business ventures and had asked her to be a part of their growth. She was very excited about the opportunity to dive into these expansion projects and felt like it was an opportunity she couldn't say no to. My heart began to race.

This felt like a breakup.

"So you want to go help them build and expand their businesses. But I thought you were vested in helping to build ours," I said. "What am I missing?"

She told me she was going to be stepping back from our business a bit. "This will be really good for you. You can really step into the forefront now. You know, Jodi . . . I cast a very big shadow . . ."

WHAT . . . THE . . .

To say I was in shock would be the understatement of the century. I was floored. I thought this was her passion and her calling too, a mutual dream of ours. An image of us brainstorming Girlfriend University together at the coffee shops and cafés flashed through my mind. Was it all just "passing the time" for her until the next big thing?

Before we could get into a deeper conversation, she said she needed to go. And so she stood up from the bench, perched on her stilettos, gathered her designer bag, and poof . . . she was gone again.

I sat on that park bench stunned.

I CAST A BIG SHADOW???

Her words rang in my head and hung in the air like an impending hurricane waiting to make landfall. It felt like she had completely undervalued me and disempowered me as a cofounder of this business. This dream. Meanwhile, she was just going to stand back and let me grow our business while she went to build another? This moment felt exactly like how Mike treated me when we were building our business. I would be doing the large bulk of the work while he sat at his laptop. I knew I couldn't repeat that pattern again, no matter what.

The next day, I reached out to Marie and told her I would like to buy her half of the business. If she wasn't interested in being a part of it, I would like to take it over completely and run with it. But she didn't like that idea. She said she wanted to continue on as we currently were, and she would just be a silent partner.

Silent partner? I knew her silence would translate to her absence. What good was this partnership if we didn't have an equality of work between us so we could really grow the company successfully?

"If you aren't vested in building this, Marie, it doesn't make sense to me to remain partners. That's what a partnership is to me . . . we set out to build this TOGETHER."

We seemed to be at a stalemate. Marie wanted to remain a partner, and I wanted an arrangement that actually fulfilled my needs of what a partnership should be in my eyes—otherwise, I might as well build the business on my own. The tense situation continued to brew, and the knot in my stomach was getting pulled tighter and tighter with every text and email.

And yes, I said every *text and email*. No further *phone calls*, no *conversations*, no *meetings*. Marie and I never spoke face-to-face again about this incredibly important topic—the future of our business. We had resorted to communicating back and forth via technology, and I knew this way of resolving conflict wasn't going to resolve anything at all. It was creating distance between us, making it easier and easier to not see the human in one another.

It wasn't long before I received an email from Marie's attorney, stating that all of the business equipment, manuals, phones, computers, supplies, and everything else be returned to Marie by week's end. She would continue to be the sole owner of Amplify U.

SOLE *owner? As in* ONLY *owner??*

In the blink of an eye, I was no longer a part of our business. Due to my lack of experience and ignorance over legal paperwork, and my trust that Marie had my best interests at heart, the company I loved so dearly didn't belong to me anymore. Technically legal, her actions stung of betrayal. And I learned an even BIGGER lesson on the importance of reading the fine print.

How could she? And WHY? I understood and recognized that Marie had put a lot of money into getting our business up and started; however, a business doesn't become successful or grow solely on the dollars put into it. It takes work, and time, and grit. And love. And none of that, from my perspective, had been present for months.

Yes, I was pissed.

But I was also so fucking sad.

Perhaps I'll never truly know the motive and reasoning behind Marie's actions. Why she seemed to retreat from our business, just when it truly was starting to soar. Why she only wanted to remain a silent partner and not my actual partner—even when our chemistry was so powerful in those early days of brainstorming. I'll never know the answer, and I'll never know what really happened for her to make that choice to become the sole owner of our company without talking to me about it first. But I do know that this moment was another lesson—a gift wrapped up in terrible hurt.

If we were "divorcing," then, just like last time, I would walk away with my head held high. I knew in my heart that her energy and attention were captured by this new venture, but I couldn't, and wouldn't, simply quit or give up on my dream of improving the lives of people and the companies they worked within. This was my passion. My purpose. And the more I thought about this "divorce" of ours, the more I realized that I didn't need anything else to make my passion and purpose come true. I had everything I needed within me.

———

I was starting over.

Again.

But I had been here before. My divorce from Mike, an all-too-fresh reminder. And despite the hurt from both of these experiences, I simply didn't want to spin in a whirlwind of ugliness and negativity. I was going to build a business with a fresh new start and a brand-new name. A name that was new to most, but as familiar as my comfiest college sweatshirt with the holes loved into it.

U & Improved: my original company name that I formed on the heels of my divorce. This time, I would rise from the ashes again, stronger and wiser.

We had a two-and-a-half-day class scheduled to begin in just five days. Students were flying in from out of state to have this life-changing experience, and I wasn't about to deny them. I was going to make it happen. Whatever it took. Amplify U may have been gone, but my company, my baby, U & Improved, was coming back bigger and better than ever!

I knew I couldn't do this all on my own—recreate my company, and plan for a class, in less than a week. I needed the help and support of one person in particular . . . someone who has had my back, and I hers, since the moment we met a decade or so prior. I grabbed the phone and made a call to Tiffany, both a best friend and business colleague of mine for all those years. She was all in to help me save these classes, these life-enhancing experiences, and relaunch this company. And within a matter of hours, we got to work.

The girls happened to be with their dad just as this was all unfolding, which was a blessing because Tiffany and I had little time to make miracles happen. There we were with papers and notes and computers and manuals strewn about all over my kitchen and living room floor. We were going to rewrite, rebrand, and redo *everything*.

Five days later, at the very start of the course, we explained to our students that there had been some big changes AND they were going to receive the same stellar experience they were counting on.

And we delivered.

U & Improved launched its first two-and-a-half-day class that Friday afternoon in early November. During those two-and-a-half days, we pushed our students, in a positive and firm way, to take a true assessment of their lives. What do they want more of? What's working and what isn't in both their personal and professional lives? We challenged them to dig deep, and we held up the mirror so they could see their greatness inside. Inspiring and helping people live their best lives is what I was born to do; it was, and is, my lifeblood. I wasn't going to let anything get in the way; nothing would stop me from allowing people to experience that "I've got this!" feeling firsthand.

The experience was incredible to witness and be a part of. To see that we were able to make this company transition happen in a matter of days, to see the class go off without a single hiccup—I was truly amazed. None of it could have happened without the blood, sweat, tears, and love of Tiffany or the amazing training team that stood by my side every step of the way.

And then, Sunday morning arrived—our first official graduation as U & Improved. I had butterflies the size of bats flying around in my stomach. We did it! We made it . . . and we were here! I put on my bright-red dress and shiny black heels (already representing our new brand colors of red and black). I had picked the girls up from their dad in just enough time to get them all dressed for the big event at the hotel where the class was held for the weekend. They were so excited to be a part of it all! As the graduation celebration was getting ready to begin, something unexpected happened. We had created quite a following due to the impact of these classes over those initial couple of years, but what I saw next stunned me.

Past graduates began pouring into the hotel ballroom. Now when I say poured, I mean POURED! One after the other, with smiles on their faces and arms open to give me the warmest of hugs. Just as I thought everyone had arrived, even more graduates piled into the room, like clowns spilling out of a tiny car at the circus. It was unreal! Tears welled up in my eyes and spilled down my cheeks.

"We're with you, Jodi," said one graduate.

"We believe in you and we believe in the work you do," said another. "You changed my life!"

"Everyone knows you are the heartbeat of this organization. Continue to build your company your way . . . with heart," said yet another graduate.

The outpouring of love, support, and belief in me, and in our classes, was overwhelming. And all that those graduates shared with me on that day was one of the biggest and best gifts of my life.

Perhaps Marie was right. She did cast a big shadow.

And now, for the first time, I was truly ready to step out from that shadow and into the light. It was my time . . . my time to help shine a bright light on others and ignite that fire within them.

And I haven't looked back since.

Dear U,

I've always found it fascinating that a chance encounter can completely change the trajectory of your life. I've been blessed to have many of these "chance encounters" (hello, Les Brown); however, one thing I have noticed is that chance encounters can be either good or bad and sometimes they can be both good AND bad. Usually, even the seemingly bad ones end up as gifts that start U on a new and better path.

What I didn't realize in my young adulthood, however, was that some people we encounter aren't always fully transparent with who they are. They only expose the bits of themselves that they want U to see. What I have come to realize, though, is that in order to have any kind of a true, honest relationship that can stand the test of time, it must begin with authenticity in our communication: showing your true self with every interaction.

Here's why we want to show our true selves, no matter what: **it gives everyone the greatest gift—transparency.** When we are transparent and honest with one another, we experience an enhanced level of communication that leads to win-win situations for everyone. My relationship with Marie could have ended so much differently had we been more direct with our communication toward each other, been more authentic with one another (not putting on a facade or being secretive or being in denial), and looked at how to create a scenario where everyone wins and no one needs to lose.

During this entire ordeal with Marie, I felt this deep pain of being cast away. Not only did it feel like I was literally being cast to the side for the sake of her relationship and her new business endeavor, but I also felt that desperate sense of isolation and abandonment: our friendship was over, our partnership was over. Once again, I was left alone to pick up the pieces. And even though she said that she cast a big shadow over me, what I learned, more than anything, was that I, too, needed to step up and step into the light. I was placing myself in my own shadow. I needed to own my OWN greatness and strength and, once again, do the difficult thing and take that first step forward, into the unknown.

Scary? Yes. Doable? Definitely. Worth it? Without question.

So here's my question for U: What are U waiting for?
It's time for U to:

Communicate your feelings to others. Being open, honest, transparent, and authentic leads to more trusting relationships, allows for deeper and more meaningful connection, and ignites a heartfelt desire to create win-win scenarios for everyone.

Express what your purpose is in your life and go after it, regardless of what others think or feel. U can't live an authentic life if U are always hiding deep within the shadows of others or yourself.

Own your greatness—however that looks and feels for U. Seek clarity and identify your own set of personal core values, and make your decisions in life and business based on those values. They are your guideposts. And when U choose to own your greatness, U show up as your best self. No one in this world is exactly like U, and that's exactly why the world needs U.

No one can ever cast a shadow bigger than U. Step out and shine bright, dear reader. And remember, U got this.

With love and gratitude,

CHAPTER FIVE

Thelma and Louise

Friendship can be found in the most unlikely of places,
if you are willing to open your heart.
—Author Unknown—

If you haven't seen the movie *Thelma & Louise*, first, you need to; second, the main takeaway from my perspective is one word: *freedom*. The final scene (I won't spoil it for you) is all about taking control of your fate and your destiny, and throughout my first fifty years, I've done quite a bit of exactly that.

I met a Louise to my Thelma many years ago, and only she and I can possibly understand the crazy trip we've been on. Neither of us would have been "friends" just from the start, as we're both so different, but the adventure we went on bonded us like nothing else.

Let me start at the very beginning . . .

———

The first time I met Mandy was around the time that Mike and I just had our second daughter together. We were at a nightclub in Orange County, one of my favorite areas of California, with its beautiful coastline views, delicious restaurants, and perfect, breezy yet warm summer weather. Mike and I were in "the OC" for a launch party event and she was one of the party's attendees. Mandy was a friend of a friend—a friend of a friend of Mike's, to be exact. Mike grew up in Orange County and always loved to talk about how he had the most amazing circle of high school friends that he was still incredibly close with decades later. Mandy was at the club with some of those lifelong friends.

Thin in frame with a big, bold smile, Mandy was a pretty woman, roughly five or six years younger than me, with a bubbly personality and an energy about her that screamed *fun*. After being introduced,

I chatted with her briefly at the event. It was just small talk, mostly about people we both knew in Mike's high school friend group, a bit about me and my girls, and a little bit about her and what she was up to at the time. It was a little hard to hear (we were in a nightclub after all) with bumping music, girls dancing on pedestals around us, and fancy martinis of every flavor scattered throughout the hands of all the attendees.

Suddenly, my husband came up to my side, smiled at Mandy, and then asked if I wanted another drink. We both said goodbye to Mandy and made our rounds to chitchat with everyone else. I remember leaving that conversation thinking how nice she seemed.

Flash forward years later to when Mike and I divorced: he decided to move out to California to be with Stacy, a woman from high school that he had fallen in love with on Facebook. And my life (obviously) was forever changed.

So while Mike was in California with a new "sort of" girlfriend, yet still living that "single guy" lifestyle, he would be out on the town quite a bit, throwing back drinks and having a good ole time. On one of those nights out, he and Mandy struck up a conversation at a bar.

Of course, Mandy thought he was an amazing guy. She remembered how charming and charismatic he seemed during her previous encounters with him, and how he appeared to be such a hands-on father, droning on and on about his two daughters. She thought to herself how he was the "perfect guy," and how one day she would love to be in a relationship with a man just like him.

What Mandy didn't know was, well, the *truth*.

————

Back in Arizona, I was doing all I could to keep food down and my two young girls alive. I wondered for hours how the heck I was going to pull us forward and out of the chaotic tornado we were spinning in. I spent countless nights awake, questioning everything I thought I knew about him and the family we had created, and what I was going to do for us now that he was gone and we were done. Endless questions with no clear answers.

Mike, on the other hand, was footloose and fancy-free, as they say. Partying and socializing and living the good life. He was spending more time with Stacy, the new love of his life. He was also spending more and more money—money that he didn't have but that he kept siphoning from his mom, Rose.

As I am sure you could have predicted, the love affair with Stacy was short-lived. Perhaps the chemistry they initially shared, that was so palpable via the internet, wasn't quite what he thought it would be once he and Stacy were spending time together in person. Ahh, the death of another fairy tale . . .

This death seemed to breathe some new life into Mike, because the next thing I knew, Mike was asking if we could meet . . . and talk.

Now, you must know that one of my commitments to myself and my girls from the very onset of my split with Mike was that I would do everything in my power to keep the lines of communication open and flowing and to always take the high road for their sake. I didn't want them to see, feel, or experience anything that would cause harm or upset them; I also kept that communication open for me as well—and my future joy, health, and happiness—in hope of coming to a sense of closure and respect for this entire relationship. So when Mike asked if we could meet at the Mexican restaurant across the street from my house in Arizona to talk, I said, "Sure."

Now, Mike's MO is to be sweet as punch when he wants something from you. His voice gets an octave or two higher, and you can see and even hear his smile through the phone when he's asking you sweetly for something he knows he is after. Knowing this, as soon as I heard that higher pitch to his voice, I assumed this meeting was to discuss wanting more time with the girls when he came back into town, or wanting me to do more of the driving back and forth from Arizona to California to make things more convenient for him. We didn't have our divorce finalized at this early stage in the process, so I ventured a guess that this was where this conversation would head. No big deal; I was prepared to talk it out and come to some sort of solution that was best for the girls.

So we met.

As odd as it seems in retrospect, the dinner wasn't as awkward as one might assume. I was beginning to come to a place of sadness for Mike. I was beginning to see, more and more, the little boy whose mother did everything for him and truly believed he hung the moon.

I saw a man that suffered from serious Peter Pan syndrome, only wanting to remain young and fun and playful, dodging reality and real-life, adult situations as best as he could. I saw, across from me at our little table in this crowded restaurant, a man nervously nibbling his chips and salsa because he knew he had fucked up, royally.

"So, I've been thinking and, well, I know I messed up."

YUP, I thought, crunching on a tortilla chip.

"We have two amazing girls, Jodi, and I think we should see if we can give it another chance." He dropped these words upon me like a freaking atomic bomb.

Is he SERIOUS? THIS *is the talk he wanted to have?* I thought it would be a conversation around scheduling, wanting more time with the girls when he came to visit . . .

I took a second to compose my answer. The restaurant was filled with its usual bustle of noise: the clatter of forks and knives, shouts of joy at a round of tequila shots, the sizzle of fajitas in a cast-iron skillet. Mike sat across from me with that sweet little puppy dog look that had always worked in his favor in the past, waiting for a reply.

"Umm, yeah . . . so . . . no. No, that's not going to happen. We've gone through hours and hours of counseling. You said you wanted to give it another chance, but couldn't stay away from Stacy. Now that relationship isn't what you thought it was. But Mike . . . we're done."

Bam. Mike drop. Literally.

Luckily, this conversation didn't happen until the very end of the dinner, because the awkwardness had officially set in. Not just awkwardness, no—his *rage* was beginning to surface through his stern look and his fidgety body posture. He was pissed. Things hadn't gone his way. He wasn't able to control me and get what he wanted.

You reap what you sow, I resolved to myself. No more manipulation. No more acquiescing. This ship had sailed and he was no longer the captain.

After I said my piece, we managed to fumble through some awkward small talk while we waited for our server to come back with the bill. I could feel his anger mounting. I knew those initial dark stares and piercing looks I was seeing between the kind words exchanged with the server. He would never let anyone else see this side of him. No, that was a side that was reserved for me. And his mom. Those on the "inside."

After we paid, we got up from the table and walked outside the restaurant toward his car. Mike gave a sarcastic and ugly "Well okay, bye," as he abruptly turned away from me and sauntered off to his car.

———

Mike couldn't be alone for very long. And the truth is he was used to having a woman in his life to take care of him. It started with his loving and much too doting mom, Rose, then it was me, and then, after he dumped Stacy, he moved on to his next victim.

Enter Mandy.

Back out on the town "living his best life," Mike and Mandy reconnected. She discovered that he was now a single dad, raising his two daughters, having to travel back and forth to see them (cue the tiny violins playing "My Heart Bleeds for You"). He built up quite a story for Mandy about how he had so much business booming in California and needed to be there, so now he had to travel back and forth to Arizona to see his children because *I* wouldn't move out there.

What business? I thought. *And you left us for another woman that wasn't all that you thought she was, realized your lunacy and lapse of any kind of good judgment, and asked me back. I said "No way, José"—I am single-handedly raising our one- and three-year-old daughters and figuring out how to get my half of this business debt paid off, while simultaneously starting a business to put food on the table and a roof over our heads, and I'M the bad guy in your narrative? Puh-lease.*

And yet, with his endless charm, endearing puppy dog eyes, and sweet voice, he got her. Mandy was officially woven into his web.

———

Months went by. I was finding my way through the pain, the anger, and doing all I could to focus on the gifts my marriage HAD given me: my darling daughters. I was still so thin, eating as much as I could manage and doing all that I could to remain positive and forward-focused, charting my new path with my young little voyagers right by my side.

It had been over ten months since our marriage imploded. It was late summer, entering into the autumn months in Arizona—still hotter than the surface of the sun. The girls and I were doing all we could to stay cool, and busy, so as not to focus on the fact that it felt like we were living in a clothes dryer. The Arizona heat had never bothered me until I became a mom looking to keep two little girls occupied all day, with no outdoor activities, besides swimming, being an option. And swimming every single day for four months was getting pretty old pretty quickly. Sometimes, to escape the pool, I'd take the girls driving on some easy errands around town. They loved going where Mommy went! And even though I constantly felt the pressure to figure out our next steps to move forward financially, I loved those summer days with nothing and no one but the three of us.

And while our summer passed in a whirlwind of brutal Arizona heat, Mike's summer was filled with his usual partying. I hadn't heard from him in a while when he called to let me know about his mom, Rose, who was admitted into the hospital because of some recent heart issues.

And so it was on one particularly hot September day, while the girls and I were driving around running a few errands, that my phone rang. Here was the anxiously awaited phone call from Mike to update me about his mom. I picked up the phone, hoping for a positive bit of news.

"Jodi! Jodi!!" he screamed into the phone, without so much as a rushed "Hello." I immediately knew something was not right.

"She fell! She fell in the middle of the night last night! She didn't call the nurse to help her to the bathroom and she fell and hit her head!"

"Slow down, Mike! I don't understand. Did you say your mom hit her head?"

"Jodi, it's really bad! I don't think she's going to make it!" he said through shock and tears.

"Oh my gosh! Okay, where are you? Are you with her?" I said, as the news was hitting me like a freight train.

"No, I can't . . . I can't go there. I'm on my way to California."

"California?? What? Mike! Turn the car around! Go to the hospital! Mike, your mom needs you!" I said in disbelief of the words I was hearing.

"I just can't, Jodi. I have to go to California. I have meetings . . ." he clamored on.

"Miiiikkkkkeeee!!!!" I screamed in desperation. I didn't care that I was sitting at a stop light and that people in their cars beside me were staring. Rose deserved a son that would be by her side when something like this happens. "Please! Turn your car around! She NEEDS you!"

"I can't. I have to go." He hung up the phone.

I was in utter awe at the fact that Rose's only son, basically her only family, wasn't going to be there for her.

I turned MY car around.

I headed back toward home. I swiftly picked the phone back up and called my dad, who promptly met me at the house to watch the girls so I could begin my action plan.

I called the hospital. I reached a nurse who told me that yes indeed, Rose had fallen and had severe internal bleeding in her head. She reiterated that this wasn't looking good and that Rose's next of kin was listed as her son, Mike.

"Do you know where he is? Can you reach him?" the nurse asked.

I was too ashamed to utter his truth.

"Yes, I have his number and have been in contact with him," I said with a quiver in my voice.

"We will need him here. Decisions are going to need to be made . . ." she continued.

Holy fuck, Mike! Why must you always run away when life gets tough? I thought, pinching the bridge of my nose and exhaling before I answered the nurse.

"Thank you, I understand. I will call him again now," I said softly.

I dialed the phone again. No answer.

Pick up the damn phone, Mike! Come ON!!! Stop running!!

I dialed again. No answer. And again. And again. And again.

What do I do? Oh my god, this is so tragic. She needs him here!

I picked up the phone again, but this call was different. This situation required me to make a difficult "call" by making another difficult call.

"Uh, hi . . . it's Jodi. Umm, yeah, Jodi Low . . . Mike's old Jodi. Or ex-Jodi. Or ex-wife," I rambled. I hadn't spoken to Mike's best friend, the best man in our wedding, in well over a year. "So, I know it's a little unusual to hear from me, but there's been an emergency and I need your help." I told him about what had happened, my conversation with Mike, and how he was headed to California as we were speaking. I begged him to please reach out to Mike right away and do anything he could to get him to turn his car around and head back to Arizona to be with his mom.

He understood and assured me he would do everything he could. He loved Rose; she had been a mom to so many of these boys as they were growing up, and I knew the news was painful for him to hear as well.

The day went on, and some more friends of Mike's reached out, as I continued to reach out to others. I was desperate, looking for someone in California to talk some sense into him.

They rallied. Some of Mike's closest friends assured me they were taking care of it, and the next thing I knew, they had Mike with them and were driving him back to Arizona. Thank God.

I did everything I could to keep myself occupied as I waited anxiously and nervously for any updates. The girls and I played Candyland and "kitchen" and watched *Little Einsteins*. I couldn't focus on much more than that. My mind was spinning with a tornado of thoughts and emotions.

What happens if she really does pass? The girls will never truly know their grandmother. And Mike! Oh my gosh, what is he THINKING? *Or why* ISN'T *he thinking? Why would he leave his mother in her most dire and desperate moments? Had he heard anything more about Rose? Did he have any updates?*

I called over to Rose's house, where I knew they were all staying, and a female voice answered the phone. I was a bit taken aback. I knew his guy friends were bringing him back to Arizona, so who was this? Rose's house cleaner, I presumed.

"Oh hi, Jodi. It's Mandy."

"Oh! OH! Mandy!" I stuttered, in disbelief once again. "I didn't realize you were here."

"Yes, a couple of the guys and I are here with Mike. Jodi, it's not good at all. We are heading to the hospital in a few minutes. Mike is going to need to make some difficult decisions," she said.

I didn't have time to process Mandy being with Mike, here, in this moment of crisis. I didn't have time to process much of anything. I knew what *difficult decisions* meant, and my heart was breaking for Rose. I remember her sitting on my couch after Mike left us, just being with me and my little girls. She was a huge part of my life, and I couldn't stand to think about what might happen next.

Rose passed away a couple of days later. Mike had made it to the hospital for her last moments and to make the difficult decision to let her go. He saw her, begrudgingly, because he didn't want to. He wanted her to be okay. He wanted to pretend it wasn't real. But it was. As much as Mike would snap at his mom and yell at her when she asked a question for the umpteenth time or "played" one of her "tracks" on repeat, deep down he loved her. She was all he really had. Rose would always tell me, "You and your family are the family we never had." She loved us so much. And she adored her granddaughters and was so excited to be a grandma. And now it was all gone.

Funeral arrangements were made for Rose. I was notified that her service and burial would be taking place the following week in California, and Mike asked if I would please attend. Of course I would be there for my former mother-in-law and for the grandmother of my daughters.

I considered what this experience was going to look and feel like. Besides the obvious emotion of grappling with the fact that Rose was actually gone, and how sad and heavy the experience of her loss would be, I also imagined walking into the funeral home with my ex-husband, his new girlfriend, and all of his lifelong friends from high school whom I hadn't seen since our divorce. I knew it might be a rush of feelings ranging from sadness to uncomfortable awkwardness, but I was okay with that. This wasn't about me, and I had gotten through many hard things before.

The following week, the day of the funeral came. I anxiously awaited my flight. Tucked in my handbag were two photos of each of my girls. I had mounted them to pink construction paper and had them draw a little picture for Grandma, and had written some sweet words to her on their behalf. I didn't know how to create closure, for me or for them, but bringing these photos and sentiments with me felt right somehow.

It wasn't long before it was time to head over to the funeral home. It was a beautiful Southern California day: the sun was out, the sky was a gentle blue, and there were flowers blooming in every shade of the rainbow. I remember thinking while driving down the streets lined by lush, green trees how much Rose adored flowers and how much she appreciated all the beauty that California so readily gives.

Once at the funeral home, however, even the beauty of the weather and the gorgeous flowers couldn't hide the palpable sense of heaviness that flooded the air. Dozens of people began filing into the funeral home and I could feel the nervous energy build inside of me.

Walking in, I immediately saw a few of Mike's friends. They gave me a small smile and looked down toward the floor—a combination of sadness and awkwardness, just as I had envisioned. It was weird, stepping into this old life of mine, with people that used to feel so familiar and warm but, in many cases, were now just *Mike's* friends, not *our* friends. I did my best to shake off the ghost of our life together and focus my attention on celebrating the life of Rose.

I saw Mike, who was doing his best to hold himself together but was visibly distraught. Who could blame him? The situation was tragic. And the only remaining family he had left was one distant cousin who was there already, sitting in the very front row.

I looked around and saw so many familiar faces: some that were warm and welcoming through all the sadness and others who didn't know what to say to me so they said nothing and looked at me from afar. I knew what they must be thinking, that Mike had never told them the real reason why we split, or, if he did, he spun the story to present him as the hero and me as the villain. *If only they knew how he had changed and distanced himself from his own family . . . and how he walked out on us for someone else.*

I began to walk toward a pew in the middle of the funeral home when Mike, standing at the end of the first pew, motioned for me to come and sit with him and his cousin in the first row. I walked over and sat next to the cousin and we caught up for a moment while Mike continued to hug guests that came to comfort him. Meanwhile, Mike's cousin softly shared her sadness in hearing about Mike and me separating and how she always thought what a lovely couple we were and how "pissed" she was at him for leaving us. It all felt like odd timing to be having this conversation, but I appreciated her sincere sentiments. Suddenly, her words were cut short when we heard some commotion and looked up to find Mike motioning for Mandy to sit with us in the front row. And suddenly, Mandy was sitting right next to me, and Mike was sitting beside her.

Well, this is awkward, I thought to myself. Here I am, sandwiched be-tween Mike's new girlfriend and his cousin, who just told me how much of a fool Mike was to leave us. This couldn't be more uncomfortable.

Until it was.

"Jodi . . ." Mike leaned over Mandy to get my attention. "I can't get up and speak. I can't do it. Could you get up and say something about my mom?"

"Ohhh, umm . . . you mean, deliver a eulogy?" I asked, dumbfounded at the request, considering the service was literally about to begin.

"Yeah, please. Thanks," he mumbled.

Did he just ask me to deliver an impromptu eulogy about my for-mer mother-in-law? Without a single second to prepare? And did he really just say that he just "can't" do it? I get it. Grief does crazy things to our brains. But I couldn't help but see the similarities between this moment and when she was in the hospital. Was he running from this tough moment too? Only to ask me, once again, to do the hard thing for him?

Mike's cousin looked at me with big eyes, wondering if she just heard what I heard, and then leaned over and whispered in my ear, "Is that Stacy sitting next to you?!"

"No," I whispered back. "That's Mandy."

"Who the heck is Mandy?" she exclaimed, in a not-so-whispery voice. I cringed, wondering if Mandy could hear.

"She's Mike's new girlfriend," I explained quietly.

"ANOTHER one?!" she exclaimed, just as the soft, somber music be-gan to play.

The service began and a priest shared with the attendees about how Rose was in a better place with no pain and suffering. Mike was sitting and listening, although after being married to him for so long, I knew that his thoughts were a thousand miles away: how this was all so surreal, how he felt it couldn't be true, how he couldn't live without his mom.

It came time for Mike to speak and he directed the priest to me with a subtle hand gesture, motioning that I would be the one speak-ing. It was all a whirlwind—everything moved so fast. I couldn't be-lieve this was my reality.

The priest appeared momentarily confused by Mike's gesture, but quickly brushed it off and moved forward as though it all had been planned. The next thing I knew, I was standing there speaking about the kindness Rose showed me from the moment we met. How she welcomed me into her home and her family, how she loved to share the story behind each of her numerous and vast collections of everything from valuable china to Beanie Babies. I retold stories of how much joy her granddaughters brought to her life, and how she was always happiest when she could be with her family. The family she always wished for, she'd say.

It was all off the cuff and from the heart. I simply spoke as stories and memories came to me. I then walked over to Rose's casket, reached into my small handbag, and placed the two photos of her granddaughters next to her, with their sweet drawings and warm wishes on rose-pink construction paper.

I took my seat after speaking and a few more friends shared their memories with those that had gathered there to remember her. The ceremony concluded and then we all followed the hearse up the hillside to Rose's grave site. Again, I was motioned by Mike and Mandy to sit in the front row at the burial. We sat there, listening to the priest and each of us "family" members were given a white rose to throw upon her casket, one by one, as they lowered it into the ground. It was beautiful; white roses were her most favorite of all the flowers and seemed like a perfect way to honor her with a final wish. I sent a wish of love and healing and gratitude to her for being such a loving mother to her son and granddaughters . . . and to me.

Just as the final roses were being tossed into the earth, I heard some commotion behind us. I couldn't see what was going on, but the voices speaking were louder—an odd and inappropriate volume for such a solemn moment. The rustle and commotion continued for a minute or two, but I did my best to drown it out, focusing my energy and attention on Rose and this final moment of her burial ceremony.

Things quieted down and the ceremony concluded. Everyone made their way to their cars. Mike was quiet with his head held low as he walked hand in hand with Mandy toward their car. I looked over and he glanced up at me and simply mouthed the words, "Thank you." I was instantly reminded of those soft and tender moments in the early days, when this was the type of loving look and gesture I would receive from him. I whispered back, "You're welcome" as I headed further down the hill toward the car.

As I continued to walk past the rows and rows of headstones, I asked some friends what all the commotion was about during those final moments of the burial ceremony. Apparently, Stacy had come to the funeral that day and arrived for the final moments of the indoor ceremony, then headed to the burial site with the rest of us. She wasn't aware that Mike had so quickly begun dating Mandy and just lost it—tears, anger—all right there at the grave site. I remembered hearing the disruption behind me, but I didn't dare turn around as I assumed it was simply a guest who was having a moment of grief, and I didn't want to draw more attention to the situation. But that wasn't the case.

As the details unfolded, I thought, *This can't be real.* Stacy was a destructive force yet again, and this time at the most inappropriate and inopportune moment. It was the ghost of girlfriends past! I couldn't help but laugh at the situation, which certainly felt good and brought a little levity to such a somber day. And yet, the reality was I couldn't believe that in such a short span of time, Mike had all three of us there simultaneously mourning his mother. Somehow, my life had become a soap opera, and I had a starring role—but Mike of course took center stage in this particular drama.

———

I've always been one to have vivid dreams. I have dreamed up quotes in my head and written them down in the middle of the night. I have been in scenarios that have felt both so real and so bizarre that I woke up breathless, wondering if the circumstance was really happening to me. Mike would tell me countless times about my sleep talking and even sleep "training," where I would think I was standing in front of a room full of people hosting a keynote or class. I was also known to be searching for files or looking for medicine or vitamins for the kids all while asleep. (Yeah, this brain goes nonstop.) The scenarios seemed so real, so vivid, even down to the dress I was wearing, that it would take me a couple of minutes to come to and realize none of it was true.

One short month after Rose's passing, I had one such dream.

It had been another busy day, juggling my time with the girls with doing all I could to get some work done on building my business idea of U & Improved. This was in those early months, before I ever reconnected with Marie and before we ever started to build our own business together. On this particular day, I had just gotten Alex to sleep (always a challenging process) and then put Iliana to bed (always a much simpler process).

I crashed that night, exhausted from my new reality, yet loving the new life I was building. As I dozed off, I was thinking about how blessed I was to have these two amazing girls and about the new chapters of this life we would write together.

I must have been asleep for about an hour when I abruptly woke. And I do mean abruptly: I shot straight up in bed like an arrow, my heart pounding in my chest like I had been running from a ferocious bear. The dream I had was so vivid, so real, so ... *weird*. I couldn't shake it. I took a few deep breaths and lay there, staring at the ceiling. *Was that real? No, it couldn't be ... okay, fall back asleep, Jodi, just fall back asleep ...*

Eventually, I did.

The next morning, I woke up, and my dream was as crystal clear as it was when I first dreamed it.

In this dream, Mike and Mandy were in California, lying in a big, modern lightwood-framed bed with gorgeous, billowing white sheets and overstuffed, fluffy white pillows. For some reason, the bed wasn't in a bedroom or even a house; instead, it was perched in the sand, on the beach. As they lay there, snuggling and happy to be with one another, ocean waves slowly began rolling up toward the bed. And then the waves grew stronger and more intense, rolling up and under their bed as they giggled and smiled so lovingly at one another, so happy to be together, yet shocked at how close this water was coming to them. It was like they were two young kids experiencing those first initial moments of puppy love, giddy with excitement and joy. But there was an undercurrent of something else too: these calm waters were brewing into a tsunami.

Now yes, it was an unusual dream, and had it been like any other night I would have just chalked it up to my brain creating some weird scenario in my head. But this little dream was different. I felt this odd connection to it and as soon as I jolted up in bed, I knew ...

Mandy and Mike were pregnant.

None of it made sense. How could I have known? The dream didn't even have a baby present in it, but I could still sense it.

I had to know if my dream was real. And I knew it was super weird to do so, but I reached out to Mike via text.

"Hey listen, I know this is going to sound really odd, but I had this extremely vivid dream and when I woke up from it in the middle of the night, I had this really strong sensation that you and Mandy were pregnant," I typed.

OMG, Jodi . . . delete, delete, delete. This is not a text you need to be sending to your ex-husband. What are you thinking?

I quickly deleted the text.

I paused.

Then I quickly retyped the text and hit send before I could stop myself again.

I waited. And waited. And waited.

A whole minute had gone by and then . . .

My phone rang. It was Mike.

"Jodi . . . I got your text. What exactly was this dream of yours?" Mike asked, sounding utterly confused.

"Okay, so I know this is so weird and sorry to bother you, but you see . . ."

I explained it all. The wood bed with the crisp white sheets, the waves rolling up on the sand underneath their bed . . .

"Jodi, just before my mom passed away, Mandy and I stayed at the Surf & Sand Resort here in Laguna Beach. We had one of the rooms right there, directly on the ocean. Remember, you and I stayed there too?! The rooms are all that light maple wood with the clean white bedding. Jodi, we just found out yesterday that Mandy is pregnant, and just yesterday we figured out the baby was conceived during our stay there, on the beach! *Jodi, how did you know?* No one knows! We haven't told anyone!" he exclaimed.

I had no answer. I had no words. How the hell did I know this from this random dream that I felt so wildly connected to? I was overwhelmed at how crazy, how downright bizarre, this all was, and at the fact that my ex-husband was now going to be a father again. I felt sick to my stomach, mad, hurt, betrayed, and sad. I wasn't really sure why all these feelings were hitting me. I guess it was all just so much, so soon. They had only been dating a few months! And now his attention was going to be divided among his two daughters, whom he left a state away, and this new family he was about to build? I hung up the phone with Mike and started pacing around the house, busying myself with whatever I could. And while I was moving around and distracting my mind from its rush of emotions, I began thinking about this new baby. I knew Mandy would make a great mother. My girls would always talk about how much fun they had with Mandy when they were out in California visiting their dad. And come to think of it, they probably talked more about the fun times they had with her than they even mentioned their memories with him. She would no doubt be a light in this new baby's life. But it all seemed odd, so fast . . .

———

The following summer, Mandy and Mike's son was born.

It was hard to fathom that this man had left his wife and beautiful baby girls, "fell in love" with an acquaintance on Facebook, and was now having a third child in a third relationship. I couldn't help but feel my heart ache for my daughters, knowing that their father's attention would yet again be shared by someone else.

Time crept on. It wasn't long before Mandy and Mike got married, their little boy present at the ceremony. The girls were not included in the festivities; they kept it small and intimate. Mike's time was getting more and more fragmented and his attention more divided. As our parenting agreement stood, I was responsible for the girls throughout the school year, and he had one week per month with them in Arizona so that they could maintain their school schedule. During the summer months, I was responsible for taking the girls to and from California multiple times, where Mike would get to spend two- to three-week blocks of time with the girls. It was heart-crushing for me to fly them out to California, drop them off with Mike and Mandy, and jump on the next flight back home without my babies. I would always come home feeling such an ache and heaviness, then would immediately run to my calendar each morning to mark a huge X on the date, just like a little girl counting down the days until Christmas.

My house had that emptiness reminiscent of those early days when the girls would spend a night or two with their dad, but now they were gone for these painfully long stretches that just ripped my heart out. I knew they were young and having fun with their dad and Mandy, who always made sure to engage in various activities that the girls would enjoy. And now the excitement of having a "new toy," this adorable baby brother, made it even more thrilling for the girls to visit. I did my best to continually focus on that and the fact that, with Mandy's help, they were in safe and capable hands.

This parenting arrangement stood in place for a couple of years, but as time wore on, Mike found it less and less convenient to come see the girls in Arizona. He would call me and yell at me, complaining about how difficult this all was for him and saying that it would be so much "better for the girls" if I moved to California too. It was a tough and painful time with all the yelling, anger, and hostility. He would explode with fits of rage over the phone. He would yell and scream at me in person, too, when picking up the girls for his weeklong visits to Arizona during the school year. His anger scared me and it definitely scared them. And no one ever saw this side of Mike; he kept it hidden, and protected, by his warm smile and his fun, charismatic charm. No one would have believed it based on what they saw. This part of him was saved for us, apparently. I hated being forced to hand the girls over to him when he came to see them in Arizona. Mandy wasn't with him; at least when she was around, I could rest a little easier knowing that there was someone there to care for my babies who could remain calm and reasonable no matter how frustrating parenting became.

A few more months went on with apparent calm, so I assumed that things were going at least a bit more smoothly for Mike, Mandy, and their son. I secretly hoped that Mandy wasn't seeing or feeling any of the same behavior I felt and saw when our baby Alexandra was born. I distinctly remembered how Mike would become more enraged as more of my attention flooded toward caring for the baby. I hoped that somehow Mandy was dodging that bullet and that, maybe now, Mike had grown up a bit and realized that he didn't need to compete with a baby.

One evening, a few years after Mike and Mandy's son was born, I got a call. Mike's name popped up on the screen of my phone. Dread always came over me when I would see his name in front of me. I never knew what I would get on the other end of the line: sweet, higher-pitched-voice Mike, who was calling because he wanted or needed something, or angry, nasty Mike, who was calling to lay into me for some reason or another.

It was sweet-voiced Mike. *Phew.*

"Hey, how are you? How are the girls?" he started.

"Good. We're all good. What's going on?" I continued, waiting to see where this could be going.

"So, I wanted to talk to you about something. Well, ask you something, actually . . ." he trailed off, still in his sweet-Mike voice.

"Okay?" The anticipation was killing me.

"So, do you think Mandy and I are good for each other?" he blurted out.

"Umm, Mike, that's a really odd thing to be asking me, being that I am your ex-wife." I said, gobsmacked. "And, I mean, how would I know? Mandy has always been very nice, but how would I possibly be able to know if you were a good fit for one another?"

I think my chin may have hit the floor at the very thought of this conversation. I couldn't believe that he was actually calling to ask me for marital advice. And I didn't know how to process it. Should I take it as a compliment, as proof I had really lived up to my promise to myself that I would do whatever I could to keep the lines of communication open, to do my best to always be kind to the girls' father, to set a good example and show them that even difficult relationships that are so hard to navigate can be tackled with enough desire? Or should I be sad that my ex-husband had no family to speak of and was beginning to alienate himself from all of his lifelong friends through his poor choices and hurtful actions?

Or should I realize that maybe I am one helluva coach for my ex-husband to seek out my advice? Nah, that thought never crossed my mind, but I did ponder this whole conversation and its possible reasons and meanings, while it was taking place.

The conversation continued. Mike went on to explain that he and Mandy were just so different from one another. He explained how she is really good with the baby, but how he wasn't sure if she was really "the one."

Was I the only one that thought this was so weird?

Apparently so.

Mike kept talking and I kept listening, feeling unsure of what my role in this conversation was or should be. It was refreshing to be talking without harsh, hurtful words, so I just went with it. It was all happening so fast I didn't know how else to react.

As we were beginning to wrap up the conversation, that gut feeling I often get when something is off hit me again.

"You know she's going to want to have another baby, right, Mike?"

"No, no . . ." he said. "We've already talked about it. We're not having any more kids. We have three already."

"Mike, trust me. Mandy will want another baby," I said again, emphatically. I felt this burning urge to make sure he heard me and could feel the conviction in my words. I just knew it. The feeling was strong. Almost like . . . she was already pregnant.

"Mike, many women want more than one child. What makes you think Mandy wouldn't want a second child of her own? And Mike, are you sure she's not ALREADY pregnant?" I blurted out.

"No, Jodi, there's no way," he said, assuredly.

"I bet she is," I said, equally assuredly.

Seriously, Jodi . . . stop your damn mouth. Why are you saying this? Like you're some kind of baby psychic or something?!

But—you guessed it—I was right. I had predicted this pregnancy too. Perhaps I was just more tuned in to Mandy or Mike or their unborn babies than even I can explain. Either way, this pregnancy led to the eventual demise of their relationship, their *marriage*. This second pregnancy created that same "run away" syndrome in Mike that he had with me. And so he fled . . . straight into the arms of yet another woman. He was running from his responsibilities, his actions, and his children. I had been in Mandy's shoes. I knew these feelings all too well and knew exactly what this betrayal felt like. I also knew the messy side of things, the logistics that swirl around co-parenting, what needed to be done for the sake of their babies, and how ugly and hard this could become for her.

As time continued to march on, my girls were getting older (they were now seven and nine). Mike's twice-a-month visits that he made during the first year or two of our divorce had now dwindled down to just one or two visits per year. Mike did insist, however, that I continue to bring the girls out to him in California, back and forth, all summer long. That is how the parenting agreement read, so I obliged. And the girls were still somewhat happy to go. There were more tears, more pleas: "Mommy, I don't want to go for so long. Mommy, please come with us and stay with all of us . . . together." It was tough—seeing how much this tugged at them ripped me apart. Yet once they were in California and could be with their dad, Mandy, and their half siblings, they were happier. So I held on to that thought and image with every drop-off, keeping the big, bright smile on my face just long enough to turn around and walk away, the tears unabashedly sliding down my cheeks.

I knew that Mike and Mandy weren't doing well. Mike was leaving for numerous trips to the East Coast on (wink, wink) "business," leaving Mandy to fend for herself with two babies.

It was all painfully familiar.

———

That summer was the very last time my girls saw their father.

No more visits. No more anything. He had checked out. Poof . . .

The Swizzler had vanished.

I couldn't figure out what was going on. *How could this be the same man that adored those baby girls when we were new parents? What in him had changed, or rather . . . snapped?*

The lavish gifts he used to send (that would upset my girls to the point they would be in tears because of the mixed messages of his gifts and his actions) had also ceased. No gifts, no appearances, no visits. It was a strange time. And when he did request for them to come to California, the girls began to beg me not to have to go see him. They were smart, and they were scared. They saw his Dr. Jekyll and Mr. Hyde behavior firsthand, no matter how much he believed he hid it from them. I did my best to reiterate the words I'd always shared since the early days.

"Daddy loves you. He's got a lot going on but this isn't because of anything you have done," I would say.

I didn't know if saying those things was helpful or hurtful. How much truth do you share with two very young girls who could never understand the magnitude of any of this? So I did my best to protect their hearts, perhaps by protecting him, in a sense. I wanted to shield their delicate hearts and minds. I hated for them to see who their father had become, but no degree of masking it helped. They *knew*. They saw it and they felt it deep inside . . . in a place even I could never reach or fully understand.

And not only could I not reach inside their hearts to comfort them often enough, but I also couldn't even reach him.

His phone had been disconnected. He was truly . . . unreachable.

What was going on . . . where WAS he? So many thoughts ran through my head, day after day, week after week. I would sit and reflect upon his actions to me, to his girls . . .

Not a dime of child support or spousal support . . . for years now.

"It's coming, Jodi." Mike would often make these empty promises. "It's just been really hard getting everything together for this new product launch. But there are huge investors who want in on it. That's why I have to get to the East Coast so much. It's gonna be big, Jodi. I'll take care of it. Promise."

Or the other version of that same story: "You have no idea the pressure I am under, Jodi. I mean, what the fuck! You aren't living a state away from your girls, figuring out how to support four kids, and fund a company, and take care of everything and everyone. You have NO IDEA, Jodi!"

The multiple levels of irony didn't miss me. I was pretty damn familiar with the magnitude and intense pressure of raising two young children completely on my own with no financial or emotional support from their father. I simply chose to not let his words, and the power he so desired to have over me, affect me anymore.

He'd spin these stories over and over and over again. Not just for months, but years. I would ask and press him. *Live up to your responsibilities! You created this!*

Nothing from him. Only anger, hostility, and blood from a turnip.

I turned my attention completely away from him and focused fully on only two things: my children and my business U & Improved.

Where your attention goes, energy flows, I would think to myself.

So I followed the advice that I gave to my clients when I coached them and I just put on the blinders that would allow me to focus on those two things and those two things only. I would often tell myself that I had to make this work. I had to figure this out. I had to continue to build this business for us, because my girls needed me, and they were counting on me.

Scratch that. *Change your language, Jodi.*

I GET to build this business. I GET to figure this out. I GET to raise these girls on my own. I GET to have all of this time with them. I GET to create a safe, loving home and environment for these little girls to thrive in. I GET to live this life; everything I have is a gift I get to unwrap.

And even as I became more determined and more empowered to figure out my life, my responsibilities, and my joys, Mike was still checked out. He was unreachable in every sense of the word now. I couldn't figure out what was going on. Why the sudden disappearing act?

But that wasn't for me to figure out anymore. This cognitive dissonance that rattled in my brain for years was coming to a close. I was strong. I was powerful. I was a leader, and I was figuring this out.

On. My. Own.

————

My closest girlfriends out in California continued to regularly reach out to check in on me and the girls. And as the true nature of Mike began to unfold, and his friends saw the truth of what was going on, those guy friends, too, would reach out and check in on us, knowing that this soap opera was going from bad to worse.

"How are you and the girls doing?" they would ask.

"How are you handling all of this? Man, this has to be so tough on you guys," they would say.

And then more details would emerge.

"Did you hear about Mike and Mandy? Can you believe it?" I didn't know the specifics, but I knew it wasn't good.

But then it got even worse.

"Jodi, we saw Mike yesterday. We saw him sitting on the sidewalk early this morning when we were taking the girls to school. Jodi, we're pretty sure . . . we're pretty sure he's homeless."

The stories would flood in.

"We saw him at the beach. He's wearing the same clothes as several days ago. He was drinking with another visibly homeless man. Oh, Jodi, what is going on??"

I had no words. I was in shock. Each tale I would hear would make me more and more sick to my stomach. What was I supposed to do—anything?

Some friends thought I'd be happy to hear he was getting what he deserved after destroying his family, hurting his now four children repeatedly through his words and actions . . .

But none of this made me happy at all.

It felt like an enormous anvil sitting in my stomach, getting heavier and heavier with each new detail and story. All I could do was remember what got me through those first shocking moments when I read that fateful text message from Stacy. I told myself I only had to remember one thing: *just breathe.*

———

The girls and I would visit our friends in California frequently over the subsequent years. The friendships I, and we, had formed over the years of my marriage and beyond only grew deeper and stronger as time progressed, because we had this strange situation in common. We would sit around like old veterans comparing war stories about what we had seen, and heard, and experienced as Mike's downfall continued.

My girls occasionally asked about their half siblings and whether they would be able to see them again. I could understand how they missed spending time with them. They were there for their half brother's birth and were able to see their half sister just a few short months after she was born.

I thought about this longing they had for this part of their family. And while there was no blood relation to me, I understood it. I came from such a small family. Growing up it was only my older brother, my dad, and my grandparents—always just the five of us. No aunts, no uncles, no cousins to play with—just us. So the desire to see this other "family" made perfect sense to me. As a child I always wondered what those big Thanksgiving and Christmas celebrations must feel like: the house brimming with energy and laughter, chaos and fun, and messes everywhere. I don't know that I ever longed for that scenario, but it certainly seemed novel and intriguing to me . . . like a whole secret world some people lived in that was so vastly different from my own. I was certain that if I were in my girls' shoes, I would be curious and perhaps yearn for that as well.

That image of my children, curious and yearning to still be connected to their half siblings, propelled me to do something I probably never would have done before. I decided to make it happen. The girls and I had a California trip planned and I decided to reach out to Mandy to see how she felt about getting the kids together. Questions like *Will this be super awkward?* and *Is this weird or wrong to be reaching out like this?* spun in my mind. But this wasn't about me, nor was it for me—this was all for my girls.

"Oh my gosh, Jodi! The kids and I would love nothing more! They ask about the girls all the time and would LOVE to see them!" she said. My heart smiled.

It wasn't "normal" or "natural" to reach out to your ex-husband's second ex-wife to begin to foster a relationship for your collective four children, but somehow it just felt . . . *right*.

———

We decided to meet Mandy and her kids at Fashion Island in Orange County, a beautiful, high-end outdoor mall that had every store and boutique imaginable, along with wonderful outdoor activities for the children to enjoy. We figured that we would meet for a while and see how things went and let the day unfold however the kids decided it should.

As we were getting closer to this visit, my girls were getting so incredibly excited. I was actually overwhelmed with emotion—and surprising joy—seeing how much love they had for these little siblings of theirs that they hadn't seen in quite some time now.

We pulled into the busy parking lot and searched endlessly for a spot. Bingo, we found one at the very end of the lot and before I could get myself out of the car to assist them, Alex was unbuckled and helping Iliana get herself out of her car seat to run and go see their brother and sister.

They ran, screaming back at me, "C'mon, Mom! Hurry!! They're here and waiting for us!" I started jogging alongside them, asking if they were soooo excited to see their siblings, to which they screamed at the top of their lungs, breathless, "YEEEEESSSS!"

We decided to meet at the big koi fish pond that sat at the edge of the mall, which was a beautiful and serene pond with large stepping stones throughout it, allowing children to walk through the pond area to get up close to the fish.

As soon as we spotted the pond, the girls kept running and ran straight into the arms of Mandy and the kids.

My heart was racing with joy, adrenaline, and a flood of emotions at seeing how much my girls truly loved Mandy and her adorable kiddos. It was so sweet, so innocent, so real. I felt so blessed in that moment to know that Mandy and I had made a conscious and deliberate choice not to let one man's behavior keep the children he helped create from having each other.

We sat at the koi pond, watching the kids play together and helping them navigate the big jumps between the stones. Inevitably, we would have a wet sandal or sock situation emerge, but it was all part of the fun. The fun of family.

"Mommy, Mommy . . . look!"

We would both look—which "Mommy" didn't matter, as these four just wanted all eyes on them.

"I can do the BIG jump!"

"Mommy, which one is your favorite fishy? I like the big orange one the best . . ."

"Can we go get ice cream now, Mommy?"

We continued to walk around that day (and yes, we got the ice cream together) and loved watching the pure joy on these four beautiful, precious little faces. The love was palpable. You could tell that there was no place any one of them would rather be.

And truth be told, while I had wondered earlier if it might feel a bit strained or awkward between Mandy and me, it didn't. As our conversations continued and lingered on that day, I knew we both could feel this was the beginning of a magical adventure—one where we could truly understand one another.

———

The girls and I began making a point of driving out to California two to three times a year to visit Mandy and the kids. We would laugh until our sides hurt at how funny they all were together. They were little clones of each other, with a definite thread of spirit that ran through each of them like a beautiful silk ribbon, tying each one to the next.

We would camp out at our hotel pool and swim with the kids. Mandy and I would open a bottle of rosé to sip on while we watched the kids swimming, and it was there we began to share our stories about our united, yet separate, paths down a very similar dark road. A road that only the two of us could ever truly understand.

It was the continuous stories of his couch-surfing from friend to friend until they, too, realized the enabling had to stop.

It was the sightings in front of a Target store, panhandling to strangers, while people he knew happened to bear witness to it all.

It was the tales we would hear of him telling people that *this* was his great comeback story—this needed to happen so that one day he could share this story from a stage. He would then be the uber-successful entrepreneur he had always dreamed of becoming, even as a young boy when he delegated his job of clipping his mother's hedges.

But there was no comeback, rags-to-riches story. No fame and glory to be had. This simply was the story of a narcissistic boy who never grew up. A man who cast two wives and his children by the wayside while he did his best to create a fictitious life that he truly believed he would one day live. And the biggest problem of all was that he lacked the work ethic to make any of it a reality. He wanted it to come easily, through the hard work of others.

I know there are two (or even three) sides to every story. I never heard Mike's version and the logic behind why he chose this path or what pivotal lesson he thought he would learn that would eventually project him into entrepreneurial stardom. But the stories I DID hear, and that I held on to, were Mandy's and mine. The conversations we had forever changed the way we viewed one another. A new, untethered compassion and intense inner strength was cultivated by two women who walked on parallel, and now intersecting, paths. These stories impacted the both of us completely. And what we concluded was that without a strong woman by his side—whether it was Rose, me, or Mandy—Mike was, quite simply, lost.

Poolside, we shared these stories and so many more. Our thoughts, our experiences, our feelings, and our realizations. While Mandy and I were so different in so many ways, this common thread we shared tied us to one another—a thread strong enough to never unravel. These stories allowed us to find our *own* story, a new narrative separate from Mike. Each time we got together, we left feeling empowered and strengthened, understanding that the impact we had on each other was something very special—so much so that a few years later I would offer Mandy a chance to take my U the Leader course. I knew she deserved to continue sharing her thoughts and experiences in a way that would powerfully transform her forever. Afterward, she told me that, because of this course, she had found her voice and was finally able to stand up to Mike when he came at her in a derogatory and condemning way. She was finally free. We both were. This Thelma, and this Louise, found each other on a journey like no other, seeking freedom from a life (and a man) that no longer served us. We found a path to a better U, and made memories to share along the way . . .

———

The trips to California became more regular and frequent. We would meet Mandy and the kids for casual kid-friendly dinners, play all day on the rides at Balboa Island, and do anything and everything else to foster these beautiful memories that the children were making together. We wanted to continue the supportive bond we had between our children, which deepened with every interaction. While we were very different women, Mandy kept me grounded in my own story, in my own experiences, and in my own convictions to stay true to myself and stay true to my kids.

The original setting of our reconnection, Fashion Island, was a favorite meeting spot, and the kids would ride the train or play near the koi fish year after year. It never seemed to get old; it was as though it had become "their spot," the place where it all began, or rather where it all continued.

As we walked around Fashion Island on one of those more recent trips (our collective kiddos now ranging in age from four to twelve), the six of us walked into a running shoe store. I was working out and running a lot at the time—a bit of an Orangetheory workout addict, I must admit—and my favorite brand of running shoes happened to have their own store, so we all popped in.

We told our sticky-faced kiddos to please not touch things inside the store—no one wants chocolate and cotton candy fingerprints on their new running shoes! Meanwhile, Mandy teased me about my Orangetheory addiction and how anyone who actually enjoyed such brutal self-torture must be *deranged*. Every interaction always felt like this: fun and easy and light.

And so while Mandy and I, and our four little (and not so little) ones, walked around the store, we were greeted by a nice young man in a crisp black polo shirt who welcomed us with a big, warm smile.

"Hi! What brings you all in today?" he asked.

"Oh, just needing to replace my favorite running shoes," I said as I smiled back at him and began poking around the large display table in front of me.

"So . . . are you all a family?" he continued with a smile.

I paused.

Mandy paused.

We locked eyes and grinned knowingly at each other.

"Yup, we sure are."

Dear U,

There will come a time in your life when U will have an opportunity to reflect on the defining moments in your life. These are the moments that feel a lot like the diverging roads in the yellow wood that Robert Frost so beautifully describes in his famous poem. When these times come, you will have a choice to make . . . a path to choose.

As in the moment when my kids expressed to me how much they missed their half siblings, I knew I had a choice to make, a decision that would forever change how they—and I—navigated our relationships with others.

When faced with any decision, it is easy to let logic take over, to make a pros and cons list and use that strong cerebral voice to come up with the "smart" choice, the choice you should or are expected to make. Time and again in my life, I have found myself in situations where I can either take the expected route, or even the easy route, rather than choose the less traveled road.

And I know these opportunities present themselves to U too.

Choose wisely, dear reader. **The easy, safe, and expected route is not always the best route for U.**

Because of our past and our defining circumstances, Mandy and I weren't "supposed to" be friends. As ex-wives of Mike's, we weren't supposed to like each other and have our children remain an active part of each other's lives. However, this singular choice to overlook what is "normal" or "expected" has been one of our greatest gifts. The most unlikely of relationships has become a genuine, lifelong friendship.

Sometimes, all it takes is a little "reframing" of our perspective, looking at a situation in a new or different way, through a different lens, from an unlikely but fruitful perspective. U may just discover that the "right" road to take is not the path U always thought U would continue to travel.

Please understand, my dear reader, that I am in no way looking to minimize the tragic and painful events that occur in seemingly all of our journeys through this adventure we call life. What I AM suggesting is that there is always something to learn, always something to gain, even from the most challenging of circumstances. U just have to be willing to look and leap in a new direction. Starting this journey of reflection isn't easy, but it begins with U:

Reflect and ask yourself the hard questions. What situation in your life has caused U stress or strife? How have U chosen, up until now, to view that scenario or event?

Give yourself the gift of a reframe. Identify those situations in your life that have troubled U and seek the lessons that came from them. What have U learned? What have U gained? Who have U become as a result of getting through them?

Walk the path less traveled and see where it takes U. New journeys lead to new discoveries. Take the path and see where it may lead to.

The reality is there is always more than one right answer, more than one way to view a situation. I can promise U this: **the way that U choose to view the things that happen to U can greatly influence the depth of joy U have in your life.**

I know this may not be how everyone chooses to view the hand that life dealt them; however, I guarantee U that the peace that reframing our life circumstances can bring is a priceless gift U will cherish forever. I know this firsthand, because even though the path of my life diverged into two roads, I chose the one less traveled, and that has truly made all the difference: in my life, my daughters' lives, Mandy's life, and the life of our unique little "family."

With love and gratitude,

the
Warrior

_____

CHAPTER SIX

Soul Family

You can tell the size of a leader by the amount of arrows in his back.
—Author Unknown—

I once read a passage in an article that discussed the idea of one's "soul family," those people in life that gather around us who are not connected by blood or by race, but through their energy and essence. These people are the family that brings unconditional love and support at the perfect time and are there during the dark times and the light.

My soul family is large, and not a day—literally—goes by during which I don't take a moment to reflect on just HOW fortunate I am to have this army of love surrounding me. My deep recognition and appreciation of these soul-family members started when I was in my thirties and really hit home for me one day when I was in one of my most favorite places in the world: the spa.

Eliza and I had been friends for several years. We met when our oldest daughters sat alongside one another in Kindermusik class, and it was in those hallowed music-filled halls that I made some of the most powerful "mom friendships" of my life. Eliza was one of those incredible moms, and whether it was introducing me to my own potential to be a coach and trainer or helping me navigate through the rubble of emotions post-divorce (both from Mike and from Marie and our business), Eliza always carried that wisdom-filled perspective, offering an additional set of eyes and that keen mind that was uninhibited in sharing her viewpoints.

One day, shortly after my split from Marie, as I was newly venturing into this business of my own, U & Improved, Eliza and I decided to meet up for a much-needed spa day. There we were, enjoying a glass of wine in the Jacuzzi at the Willow Stream Spa in one of Scottsdale's most luxurious resorts. I remember feeling guilty spending money on myself and treating myself to this spa day when there were so many other areas of my life needing and deserving my attention and my money. However, I had learned early on after my divorce that I was no good to anyone or anything if I didn't take care of me. So I let my guilt subside with each sip of my glorious wine and focused my attention on this time carved out with my dear friend.

We sat and relaxed among the bubbles, enjoying the soothing spa atmosphere that somehow made me feel like we were far, far away from our real "mom" lives. We talked about our children, our own childhoods, our dreams for our futures, our dreams for THEIR futures, and every imaginable topic in between. It was a therapy session of sorts, right there in the Jacuzzi.

We began talking about the tidal wave of craziness I had experienced leading up to this spa day, from Mike to Marie and everything between. It had certainly been a whirlwind, to say the least.

In a quiet pause in conversation, Eliza said, "I have a question for you."

"I'm all ears, girl," I said with a smile.

She set her plastic, pool-friendly wine glass down and stood up.

"So, Jodi, you live like THIS . . ." she said emphatically, as she raised her arms into a sort of goalpost position, while smirking and slightly pointing her chin up to the sky.

Hmm, okay, I thought. *There's some validity to that.* I have always lived with my arms wide open. No matter what challenges me, or pushes me, I still have a "let's do this" type of attitude. Whatever it is, I tend to love living with my arms wide open and seeing where the path takes me.

"But, Jodi, I live like THIS . . ." she said, as she crossed her arms in front of herself, almost like a shield. "You trust *everybody*! You let everybody in, and then inevitably, you get hurt. Why do you keep doing that to yourself?"

I was about to speak and then stopped. And I pondered for a few moments both the complexity and depth of her question.

I HAD been hurt . . . a lot. I have had a series of people close to me leave me or hurt me since my childhood. *Why DO I do that?* I wondered to myself.

"You know, it's a great question. And I really need to take some time to reflect on it, because there's a lot to think about," I said. "But my immediate rationale is this: I always assume the best in people.

And I guess I always expect the best FROM people too. I feel like there is good in everyone, and I am on this intense mission to find what that 'good' is. But you're right, lots of times on that quest to see and believe the best in people, I trust too easily and I get hurt . . .

"Badly," I added.

"I know you always assume the best in people, Jodi, but it doesn't seem to be worth all the hurt you go through because of it," she added.

We continued on to discuss some of those recent hurts and disappointments, not just in my life, but in both of our lives, and while the conversation moved forward and the day carried on, as did the weeks and months thereafter, my memory of that conversation has stuck with me for years and years.

I have come to this conclusion, after literally *hours* of contemplation on that one direct and ever-so-thought-provoking question:

I CHOOSE to live this way. And while my life might be easier if I played it safe and didn't let others get too close, that's simply not me. My choice is to live with my arms spread WIDE open, inviting others into my life and my heart. And if arrows come my way? So be it. I'll pull each of them out, just as I have countless times before. And I will learn the lesson that I was meant to learn from my interaction with them.

Naive? Maybe. But ME? Absolutely. And I wouldn't—and couldn't—have it any other way.

———

By all psychiatrists' definitions and diagnoses, I am sure that I should have some kind of "abandonment issues." Not just because of my divorces (both personal and professional). No, this sense of *abandonment* pattern started much earlier in my life than that.

My parents got married after college. They met in the language lab at Syracuse University. My dad was a young man full of energy and optimism completing his degree in interior design and fine art, while my mother was a beautiful and brilliant Fulbright scholar who was an exchange student from the Netherlands. I imagine there must have been a pretty strong connection during the early days of their budding romance across that language lab, and I imagine that as a young, bright woman, my mother must have felt sure that this relationship was a sign that she was meant to be here.

My parents got married in Holland after college and began charting their path through life together. They decided to settle in Upstate New York, where my dad was born and raised by my grandparents, who had immigrated there during World War II to escape Hitler.

They lived in a beautiful home, off the land my grandparents owned, which originally housed their dairy farm. The house had a long driveway down to the main road and another driveway that veered to the left, joining it to the driveway of my grandparents' house. They were next door neighbors.

Now, perhaps that was a recipe for disaster for a young couple looking to start their life and family together, or perhaps it was a blessing, being so close to doting grandparents who could help a young mother who was new to the country, to marriage, and to motherhood. Either way, as my parents started their lives together, their partnership began to unravel. As a young woman and immigrant, my mother must have missed her family and homeland, and perhaps her sense of freedom, now that she was immersed so heavily in this "new" family with her in-laws a stone's throw away. And I am certain that my dad was doing all he could to juggle keeping his young wife happy while he, too, was navigating fatherhood and simultaneously creating art and design projects to advance his career. It couldn't have been easy with all the variables in play. And while a new marriage and having children changes everything about what life looks like, my dad couldn't possibly see what was around the bend.

My mother ended up having an affair with the husband of a couple they were best friends with. Yeah, super weird. That clearly was the beginning of the end for both of those marriages. My grandparents, understandably, were furious and very protective of their only son, and their only grandchildren, and a nasty divorce ensued. I am sure that my grandfather, being the patriarch and the protector, wanted to do all he could to keep his small family intact—which meant having my mother leave our home after what she had done. Given that both of my grandparents had experienced such inexplicable trauma and loss in their own past—losing family members, their homes, their lives as they had known them, while escaping Hitler—their deepest desire was to keep everyone as safe and connected as possible. The hurt my mother caused was just too much to repair.

My brother, who is six years my senior, has memories of this time that are much clearer than mine, as I was only two years old. We would spend countless hours at my grandparents' home playing, using our imagination to create games. Fun, creative play was a cornerstone of our childhood. My grandmother would cook amazing dinners each night for all of us, her parents included, so it was a home full of generations. While my memories of this time are faint, what I do recall, quite vividly, are the visits I would have to make to see my mother, who now lived in New Jersey.

Because my brother was about nine years old at the time, and I was only three, he had been deemed old enough to testify in court about his desire to *not* have visitations with our mother; the court allowed him to forgo those visitations, which was pretty unheard of for the mid-1970s. But that wish of his was granted. I, on the other hand, was far too little to make a decision of that magnitude, so the courts determined that I was to visit my mother in New Jersey on the weekends.

I distinctly remember my mother pulling up to the very end of the driveway and having to walk down the long driveway to meet her, my little red leather suitcase in tow. I would get into the front seat of her bright-red Gremlin and off we would go to New Jersey, a seemingly long and adventurous drive away. As soon as we began driving, I remember, my mother would pull out a giant one-pound bag of M&M's and let me eat those to my heart's content, unbuckled in the front seat, at age three. (It's still mind-boggling to me to think about how people's faces would drop in horror if any parent drove like that with a child today!)

I don't recall much of the conversations on those car rides. I simply remember brief moments of my visits with her. For instance, I remember Sasha, the cocker spaniel puppy she bought to entice me to visit more often. I remember the fireflies that would flitter around in the evenings and my wish to collect them all in a jar. I remember sitting in an attorney's office, afraid to look at her lawyer, who was doing his best to get information and answers from me about my level of happiness, and spinning my chair around so the tall, upholstered back of the chair was the only thing he and my mother would see. I remember my mother's bright-blue glass Noxzema jar, filled with the purest white magical potion that she would apply religiously to her face each night . . . and the little green and white stool I would use to climb up to look at said jar and stare at its beauty. Back with my father, I remember insisting that I only sleep in the twin bed farthest from the window, petrified that she would kidnap me in the middle of the night.

I remember my mom spending time on her loom, creating weavings, as creating art was also one of her passions, much like my dad. She would allow me to take bits of fabric and put them into the loom all by myself, and I remember feeling like such a big girl!

I remember dragging my suitcase up the long driveway from the main road all the way to the house because my mother told me she couldn't take me any further—that my family wanted to hurt her.

I remember my mother's new husband lying next to her in bed, sleeping without a pillow, and wondering why he chose to sleep like that, and equally wondering who he was. And how, as I lay next to my mother, I would stare at her moles and freckles and get excited seeing how I could trace my finger down her arm to connect all the dots.

I remember being so scared to go to kindergarten and asking my grandfather to promise to be the very first car in the pickup line, afraid, again, that my mother would snatch me up from school and take me away from my family forever.

These memories are all snapshots, brief moments captured in my mind like Polaroid photos. No context, no connectivity, per se— just short moments and images; the "highlight reel" of my very early years of childhood, collected there, unsorted and stashed away in my mind's eye.

And yet, some of these memories clearly weren't the highlight reel of my childhood. Many of these memories were the lowlights. The VERY lowlights. The fear, the confusion I felt when I was around her . . .

The truth is I never had a mother. These few memories—they don't make up what it means to be a mom. They could never atone for the lack of a mother figure in my life and for missing out on experiencing the joy that a mother can bring to her children—the very beautiful, awe-inspiring little lives she brought into this world. This was a feeling I never fully understood until I was on the other side, as a mother myself.

And so, while I never really had a mother, what I did have was one hell of a father, a brother, and grandparents.

And luckily, as fate and life would have it, I ended up finding a "mom" along the way.

———

My dad met Suzanne through the elementary school that my brother and I, and her two children, attended. My dad and Suzanne had some things in common right from the start: they were both divorcées, and both highly engaged, loving, and involved parents. Suzanne was a gorgeous woman with the most striking and stylish short haircut that always looked so cutting-edge, even back in the '80s. And my dad, always warm and outgoing, an artist into aesthetics and beauty, not only found Suzanne beautiful on the outside, but, most importantly, beautiful on the inside.

They began dating when all four of us kids were in school, and through their relationship, we all became very close. The six of us would go out to Swensen's, our favorite place for ice cream, and laugh until we snorted and cried, a hallmark of time well spent together. We would celebrate birthdays, Hanukkah, Christmas, and Valentine's Day together, always laughing, joking, playing, teasing, and outsmarting one another.

The annual Valentine's party at Suzanne's house was by far everyone's favorite occasion of the year. We all got into it, wearing red, white, or pink clothes, adorned with heart-shaped jewelry and headbands. The more "love" we wore, the more love we seemed to feel. And Suzanne's house was always filled with love, Valentine's Day or not.

There is really only one way to describe these Valentine's Day parties: they were *epic*. Suzanne's beautiful, white lacquer dining-room table would be completely covered in red, pink, and white Valentine's decorations. An old-fashioned Valentine carriage, made completely out of paper, would be the traditional focal point of the table, surrounded by swirls of curling hot-pink, red, and white ribbon scattered about the table. Red and silver heart-shaped confetti would be strewn across the table, adding even more sparkle and love.

And then came the food.

Heart-shaped hamburgers were grilled and served on custom-made heart-shaped buns. Broccoli and tomatoes were laid in a perfect, giant heart shape and served on a beautiful white-porcelain platter. Of course, the heart-shaped ice cream cake, covered in light-pink marshmallow frosting and decorated with red heart-shaped candies was the grand finale for dessert. Once we were adequately stuffed with love, both literally and figuratively, it was on to *Categories*, our favorite family game in which we four kids would do WHATEVER it took to outsmart and outwit one another and our parents to prove that WE were the smartest, most creative, and by far most clever kid.

The game simply involved listing five agreed-upon categories and five letters of the alphabet, much like the modern game *Scattergories* (we were so cutting-edge, we played it before it was an actual game!), and let me tell you, the level of ingenuity and fierce competition that abounded would make both world-class scholars and Olympians proud. It was intense; oftentimes, we would have to take some of the most creative (or perhaps "far-fetched") answers up for a vote. And getting a thumbs-down around the Valentine's *Categories* table was far worse than anything Simon Cowell could say to you on some talent-based TV show. (The original) *Categories* is still a family favorite to this day, having now been passed on to my own children to enjoy.

During every party or big life event that each of us kids experienced, Suzanne was there to cheer us on or dry a tear. And during a Valentine's party at Suzanne's home, she was of course the hostess with the mostest, always making sure that everyone was well taken care of, from full glasses and bellies to happy, joy-filled smiles across our faces. But along with the joy and the fun, Suzanne also challenged us. She pushed us to keep learning, to defend our most obscure and insane *Categories* answers, to be loud and authentic and *us*. And now, as an adult, I know that those tiny moments around that beautiful, shiny white table were all chosen purposefully to encourage us to speak our minds, to defend our beliefs, and to push us to continue to grow.

Suzanne was, and still is, always there for me. She has always been the most wonderful maternal figure for this "girl with no mama." She gives me the perfect trifecta: an active and engaged listening ear; a genuine interest in and love and care for what I am saying and feeling, coupled with her spot-on "makes you think deeper" line of questioning; and, finally, the sound and sage words of wisdom that only a mother can share. Above all else, she was also there during the tough times, from when she coached me through the bathroom door about how to properly use a tampon to my divorce from Mike, and every-thing between. Most recently, Suzanne was there to help me with the details of my grandmother's passing, making sure no boxes were left unchecked.

During the entire journey, she was there, saying things like, "Jodi, dear, I am simply calling to tell you that you will want to order eight to ten copies of the death certificate. You will need original copies as you wrap up Omi's affairs, and they won't accept photocopies, so just be sure to order more originals than you think you will need."

It's things like that that make Suzanne so special to me. The things that a mother shares with her daughter because she has traveled down this road before; she knows what to look for, what to expect, and she prepares her daughter with the tools she needs to navigate her own journey successfully. Now THAT's a true mom.

Over the years, I've learned so much from Suzanne that I have incorporated into my own life. For example, the art of entertaining, which simply means that everything special in life is cause for cele-bration. To this day, whether it's the colored icing on my daughter's birthday cake or the personalized invitations for U & Improved class graduates, I celebrate with those sentimental details that show the meaning of relationship and connection.

Another lesson I put into practice continually is to be that listening ear when others need it most. Suzanne taught me how to actively lis-ten, to make every person feel like they are the only person in the room that matters. She asked questions that allowed me to probe deeper, like "Well, how do YOU feel about that?" or "What do YOU think that means?" Today, active listening is a crucial part of my U & Improved classes and coaching. Especially with our U the Communicator partic-ipants, we both teach and infuse Suzanne's style of deeper questioning into every interaction to create real connection. Even my daughters appreciate this lesson. I am certain that my girls and I have the depth of relationship that we do because we practice active listening and do our best to really HEAR each other, not simply talk over each other or demand our ideas or viewpoints get across. Whether it's helping my girls with a problem at school or getting to a deeper understanding of their own goals and motivations for their lives and futures, I know that being 100 percent present and asking them to identify how THEY truly feel—what their guts and hearts say—is the key. And so much of that wisdom came from Suzanne.

Finally, Suzanne taught me that talking about and dealing with uncomfortable things is simply a part of life. All of us must sit down at the white lacquer table and open up with one another if we are truly to become family. I remember the phone call she made just recently, as I was tidying up all of my grandmother's affairs, simply to say, "Jodi, dear, you know you don't have to do this all on your own. It's okay to ask for help." And if anyone knows me, they know that I love to do, do, do and have the mindset that I truly can accomplish anything. And for the most part, I have done things all on my own, as that's the way my life has unfolded in many regards. But hearing those words echoed back to me during such a painful time in my own life felt like a good, long, nurturing hug. This gentle reminder from Suzanne helped me to slow down and deal with difficult things with the help of others. That's a huge lesson on leadership that we teach in our U the Leader class when we hear and see great leaders feeling the overwhelming burden of feeling as though they must have all the answers and must have that *I've got it all handled and under control* mentality. We teach them that asking for support is not a sign of weakness but a sign of strength, for it is what allows others to feel useful and helpful and a part of something bigger than themselves. (Not to mention that asking for help and support means that you, as a leader, are humble enough to lean on the strengths of others and that you are someone who truly chooses to play as a team.) My own lesson taught back to me; a powerful reminder that I am not alone.

It's funny, but in reflecting back to when I was a little girl, I wasn't into playing with dolls or babies; instead, I played "office." I set up a makeshift desk in my grandparents' guest bedroom closet, with my yellow plastic phone and receipt books galore, selling my Pop Bead jewelry to imaginary customers. I loved writing up their imaginary transactions in my "ledger," while carefully wrapping up their purchases and sending them on their way. I felt so grown up serving my fictitious clients, who in my mind were just as real as the sun in the sky. Little did I know that serving my clients and playing "entrepreneur" would be the path I would end up charting as an adult. And despite not being into dolls, one of my earliest memories is of telling myself that when I became a mom one day, I was "gonna be the best mom EVER!" just as I had the best Pop Bead boutique ever. I remember feeling a deep, burning passion inside every time I thought about this idea. Even though I hadn't grown up with a "true" mom, and I knew there was no manual for this job, I knew from such a young age that one day—someday—I would do this and I would do it well, no matter what. When Suzanne came into my life, I saw a mom in action, and while my thoughts about mothers back then were generally more of confusion, abandonment, and feeling left behind, Suzanne changed all that and gave me compassion, support, and reliability. Now, don't get me wrong: my father, brother, and grandparents did an exemplary job at doing all of that and more as well, but for a young girl, having a mother figure is different, and vital. My determination to be that great mom and seeing and FEELING Suzanne model that for me throughout my life has helped me have the strong, open, and trusting relationship I have with my daughters today. And for that, I am eternally grateful.

Throughout my life, I have come to realize that finding those true connections—like with my Suzanne—can create an impact that lasts. When you find your tribe, whether that's your family that you were born into, the family you create along the way, or a hybrid of both, that tightly woven fabric of love and true support will exponentially grow your belief in your own potential. When you can see true potential in yourself because of your supportive tribe, you can then see the impact you can make on others in the future. I know it did just that for me. And while it's been said that you can't pick your family, I have found that some of my most beautiful relationships have come not from the family relations I was born into but the family I have found and nurtured along the way.

This is why, when Eliza pointed out that I lived with my arms wide open no matter what happened—abandonment, betrayal, hurt—I consciously decided that I would continue to CHOOSE to live that way. I realized that if I didn't live with my arms open wide, I would miss out on some of the most treasured relationships, from Suzanne to Eliza to all my other treasured friendships. Yes indeed, family can come from all sorts of places, and I was just lucky enough that my father met this bonus mom all those years ago, back at Kiva Elementary School.

Who would have thought that the little girl with the big red suitcase, and no real mom to call her own, would someday find a unicorn mom of her own.

Dear U,

When my dear friend asked me so many years ago why I live with my arms wide open, given that I continually seem to get hurt by others, it made me stop and think ... for **years**. It's still a point of reflection for me to this day because it has allowed me the space to truly look inside myself and figure out why it is that I choose to live this way, regardless of the possibility of hurt happening.

Regardless of my answer to that question, what's most important right now is for me to ask U the same: **So, dear reader, how do U choose to live?** Arms wide open or arms clenched tightly around yourself in protection? While there's no right or wrong answer here, U need to know that, either way, it's a choice. **No one decides FOR U how U choose to show up and live your life**—that choice is ultimately up to U.

And that raises the next question: **Who do U let in?** And how do U know it's "safe" to do so? Listen, I'm not the best person to ask on that one because, let's face it, I have trusted often and gotten burned far too often along the way. But I wouldn't change one bit of it. Because what I've discovered from that soul-searching question is that if I didn't live with my arms wide open, I would have missed out on some beautiful relationships and the chance to choose my tribe.

So while we might want to ask *Who do I let in?* the real answer lies in trusting yourself to live openly and deeply with someone until that someone gives U due reason not to.

Because here's the truth about relationships: **if U don't let others in, U will never know the extraordinary people U may meet and the life-changing relationships U might have**.

Had I not met Mike and let him into my life and heart, I wouldn't have my two amazing, breathtaking, awe-inspiring daughters. Had I not trusted Marie in those early days of my career, it wouldn't have led me to develop my company, U & Improved, which is my life's passion and purpose. Had my dad not been open to socializing with the other parents at the elementary school looking to meet people in a new state, I wouldn't have the mom I have in Suzanne. The thought of not having any one of these three things in my life makes me shudder.

Ultimately, **when it comes to choosing your tribe, you must trust—**

and verify. Like I have told U before, believe people when they show U who they are but, first, trust in yourself enough to allow them into your life in the first place.

And once U let them in, the ones that are meant to stick will stick because you've followed the protocol that my dear "mom" Suzanne taught me:

Every person U care about is worth celebrating. Go all in and pull out all the stops for those U love, both at home and at work. This isn't about the money U spend; it's about the feeling U cultivate. Feeling love and a sense of belonging are basic human NEEDS, so create that feeling for those amazing people in your life, and do it up right.

Listen . . . actively. None of this surface-level bullshit. Enough of that. The half-listening, typing while you're talking to someone, or someone else looking at the TV while U are wanting to share something that's on your mind and heart? No. Just . . . no. Don't do it. Turn off the distractions, make eye contact, and seek understanding in your conversations. It's the only way it works. The people in your life deserve it, and so do U.

Get comfortable being uncomfortable. Life is ever changing. If U walk into a hospital and U see a heart rate monitor going up and down, that's a good thing—that's LIFE! Life IS the ups and downs, the highs and lows. What we don't want to see is a flatline! So throw your arms up, enjoy the ride, and when difficult moments occur, as we know they will, lean on all those beautiful hearts and souls U were brave enough to allow in. This is your tribe, your collection of chosen and unchosen family. And the funny thing about life? U can't do it alone. So use your resources and be there for these people when they need U—because they will need U and, inevitably, you will need them too.

A phrase we say a lot in our U the Warrior class is, **"If U want to go someplace fast, go alone . . . if U want to go far, include others."**

I want U to go further faster. So open yourself up to let others in, trust and verify along the way, and enjoy this crazy roller-coaster called life.

With love and gratitude,

CHAPTER SEVEN

Eclectic Wisdom

*There are only two ways to live your life. One is as though nothing is a miracle,
the other is as though everything is a miracle.*

—Albert Einstein—

I come from a strong lineage of brave, powerful, bright, and independent people. And I love that.

Being the granddaughter of Holocaust survivors who had to leave everyone and everything they knew to start their lives in a foreign country, with their family suddenly just ripped apart, I could feel throughout my childhood both their love and their need for my protection. Which meant I grew up in a bit of a proverbial bubble.

I remember being told to always wear shoes in the house so that I didn't step on a piece of glass. I wondered how so much glass could be dropped as to create the intense need for constant shoe wearing, but I never really questioned it. That was just one of my grandparents' house rules. Another house rule was that I wasn't allowed to ride my bike outside of my grandparents' cul-de-sac so that I was safe, and while it was a bit dizzying riding around in circles, again, I just went with it.

Now, this little bubble I was raised in wasn't "bad"; it was simply different. And I never felt hindered or held back by these protective boundaries, I just felt *loved*. I was loved by three adults—my father, my grandmother, and my grandfather—who wanted their little girl to be safe and sound and happy. And with an older brother as a playmate and trusted confidant, my life was pretty darn good.

As an adult, I have recognized the incredible amount of wisdom these four individuals instilled in me, and how those learnings shaped me into the woman, mother, entrepreneur, coach, and speaker I am today.

We were the Fab Five in my mind: me, my grandparents (Omi and Opi, as we called them), my dad, and my older brother. And while we were three generations, we always acted as one collective unit—one family.

Both of my grandparents were born in Europe. My Opi was born in what was then Poland, and my Omi was born in Vienna, Austria. Both were considered Austrians; however, that was something my grandfather would later denounce once his country became what it did during and after World War II. Once Opi came to America, that was, and would forever remain his homeland, to the extent that he would never even consider purchasing anything but an American made car and would physically bend down and kiss the ground in the airport when we landed back in the States after our trips abroad. He was disgusted with Austria and Germany and all of those that allowed Hitler's reign to occur, and his passion for his new country was immense.

My grandfather was also a lover of knowledge and a lifelong learner. As a little girl, I remember how every morning he would wake up at around 4:30 a.m. and head to his favorite breakfast place in Scottsdale, Arizona, where we lived, to have a bite to eat and a cup of coffee. My grandfather was very loyal—a man of few friends but those that he met and truly connected with he held dear. And while I tend to have a much broader circle of friends that I hold near and dear, we both shared a love of ritual and routine. My Opi would go to the same little café each morning and talk with the staff there that knew and loved him, and then he was off to one of two places: When my brother and I were younger, if it was a school day, he came over to our house early in the morning to wake us up and make us a little breakfast (generally a Pillsbury Toaster Strudel; if you know, you know—they were the bomb back in the '80s) before taking us to school. If it was a weekend, it was off to the library for my Opi, where he would research and read the works of great philosophers, from Socrates to Plato, Aristotle to Goethe. He would read and take copious notes in his black notebook, writing down the gems that really struck a chord with him. And those quotes would become the backdrop of my childhood . . .

"Jodi, always remember, a black or a white horse is not a horse, a horse is a horse," he would repeat.

"I know nothing . . . but because I DO know nothing, I know more," he would share.

Profound quotes and sayings from great minds were his passion, as were learning, growing, and sharing this wisdom with others, mostly my brother and me. And while I generally didn't know what he was talking about as a little eight-year-old girl, the repetition of these quotes became the foundation of MY love affair with words, language, and bigger thinking. (You've probably noticed quotes have even made their way into every chapter of this book.) There is just something about the beauty, depth, and playfulness of words, the way language can make a reader feel or a listener understand themselves and the world more deeply. To this day, language continues to move me. Deep meaning hidden between sentences and the clever use of words or a turn of phrase simply makes me giddy. A little weird, I know . . . but I can't help it. Words are my jam.

And words were Opi's jam too. His love of language and philosophy was coupled with his love of history and wanting to be the change in the world. He believed deeply and passionately that humanity would be the destruction of humanity if we couldn't collectively come together and support one another with less division and more equality. Seeing his family torn apart during World War II, and living through such a dark and painful time, created not only his protective nature, but also his desire to preserve their memory while simultaneously eradicating the future of such hate. The moment when I saw this come alive in him has always stuck with me.

When I was fourteen years old, the five of us headed on a big trip to Europe. With way too much luggage in tow, we set off to see a good handful of countries, one of which was my grandparents' former homeland of Austria.

Not only did we get to walk the streets my grandmother, my Omi, would walk as a little girl and see the masterful *Stephanskirche* (St. Stephen's Cathedral) that stands as the proud seven-hundred-year-old icon in the heart of the city, but we saw some of the smaller shops and places she used to visit when she was a young girl. We didn't see the sights simply as tourists, but rather through Omi's and Opi's own eyes. On that trip we even went to visit my Omi's childhood home in the country, finding in the old torn down house just one remaining intact piece of the oven they would use to cook their meals.

It was an incredible trip, filled with history, and stories, and of course lessons to learn from my family's rich past having lived through so much there. But the moment that has forever been etched in my mind was walking through Mauthausen, the concentration camp that took Omi's uncle's life.

I remember walking hand in hand with my grandfather, his long white hair stirring ever so slightly from the breeze that day. It was a dreary and overcast day—weather perfectly suited for the ominous feeling of the camp and the heaviness in all of our hearts. We had walked through the barracks and seen "the showers," the gas chambers that killed thousands of innocent human beings. We meandered through the museum that housed the painful images and relics of days that should be erased from the future but never forgotten in our minds and hearts.

Once we ventured outside, as I walked in step with my grandfather, it all really hit home. There in front of us stood a powerful sculpture that I will never forget. A gargantuan bronze representation of a man, dressed in the bleak uniform the prisoners were forced to don, a hollow, gaunt face with closed eyes and arms raised up partially as if to say, "I want so deeply to fight for this life I was given, but I am tired, and weak, and frail . . . I have no more fight to give." Even at fourteen years old, I saw and felt the agony of all those stolen lives.

We both stared at this statue and as we looked at this powerful image in front of us, surrounded by the perfectly fitting cold, damp air and gray, looming clouds, I saw my grandfather, my pillar of strength, simply break down. The tears streamed down his cheeks and his body shook ever so slightly as I hugged him with my small arm wrapped around his waist. It was something I had never seen before and would never see again.

He wept, standing outside in the cold, the tears continuously trickling down his face.

"Always remember, my Jodi. Always remember . . ." he said to me in a whisper.

I remember that moment so clearly, feeling so sad and scared. I had never seen this giant of a man, in my eyes, in such a vulnerable place before, and my heart ached for him. And with him. And for my sweet Omi, who had lost her uncle because the Nazis chose to use him to build the *Todesstiege*, or "Stairs of Death." The prisoners were forced to carry blocks of granite, weighing well over one hundred pounds each, on their backs, up the 186 stairs in a line, one prisoner behind another.

All day. Every day. The prisoners would ultimately succumb to the weight of the stones and the relentless pressure on their frail bodies, causing them to be crushed by the stones and creating a domino effect of death. Prisoners would die daily on those stairs. My great-uncle was one of those men, tortured on those stairs, until one day when the Nazis decided to officially end his life by removing him from that task, and instead, using his malnourished and weak body for medical experiments.

Revolting. It was enough to make me sick. Looking at the photos in the museum and knowing my family—my blood—was among those hundreds of men carrying those stones . . . The image is forever ingrained in my mind and my psyche. The eeriness of walking around the barracks, seeing the gas chambers, and stepping on those gray cobblestone streets, knowing what had happened exactly there just forty or so years prior, was heart-wrenching.

But the image that has forever stayed with me—that forever changed me—was the deep, heartfelt moment of seeing my crying Opi and being there to comfort him as we stood there in the cold, damp air.

His appreciation of our family, of what they had been through, of all of those that never made it out and back to their families . . .

His desire to show me how inhumane we can be to one another and to fight passionately to show people a different way . . . a way of love . . .

I believe we all were forever changed that day, our hearts just a little bit heavier, carrying around the weight of our family's past. Yet, for me, it was also the day that my heart was cracked open with possibility. The day that I realized I wanted to, and *had* to, somehow be a part of a change in the minds and hearts of humanity. A change for the better.

This experience with my Opi came full circle for me just a few years ago as I was doing some spring cleaning and sorting through a slew of old boxes in my garage.

I opened up an old box labeled "Books," finding some old classics mixed in with some travel books and even a couple of old textbooks. I began sorting them, deciding which to keep and which to donate, when one small book, resting on its spine, caught my eye.

The Diary of a Young Girl by Anne Frank.

There it was. A book I hadn't seen in over thirty years. The book my Opi gave to me when I was a little girl, and he made sure I read it, and understood it, and felt it. I remembered the profound impact this sweet young girl's words had on me back then; somehow, I felt like we were related—we were family through our shared heritage. And I instantly was taken back to that trip to Mauthausen; that visit made it all come to a painful light for me just a few years after I had read her diary, the words of her life. As I blew some dust off its cover, the corners of the book a bit weathered and torn, I opened up the old book and was startled to see an inscription—one that I hadn't remembered was there.

"Jodi dearest, Always remember what inhumanity has done to innocent humans by members of the human race! Love you, Opi. —1/11/1982"

As tears filled my eyes, I was instantly taken back to those moments at Mauthausen, holding his hand and hugging his waist as he wept. I felt the rush of emotions I'd felt decades prior, as if they were all happening for the first time there on my garage floor.

My Opi taught me to be a passionate warrior. To stand up for those that don't have a voice, those that have been disenfranchised or have been made to feel "less than." He taught me to fight for all of those things that I believe in, to always remember history—and our history—and to never take for granted the freedoms we have, because so many others don't have that freedom or were simply never given that chance to experience it in the first place.

And I can't help but think, as I share this story with you exactly forty years after he wrote those beautiful words in that book for me, that none of his words and teachings have gone to waste.

———

My Omi was about five feet tall, although if you asked her, she would say she was five feet five inches, which I truly think she believed she was. She was small in stature but enormous in presence ... a mighty little lady with the heart of an angel.

My grandmother grew up in Vienna with all of the luxuries, very similar to the life portrayed in *The Sound of Music*, for all of you movie aficionados. Perhaps the most memorable of the luxuries, at least as it appeared to me as a young girl hearing about her childhood, was that Omi had a governess, a lady who helped raise her and her older sister. (Fun fact: I was lucky enough to meet Marianne, my grandmother's governess, on two occasions when visiting Austria, although I only understood some German and couldn't speak much of it, and she spoke zero English. For some reason, though, that didn't seem to matter to either of us. I think we both were just so happy to make each other's acquaintance, knowing all that my grandparents had managed to live through.)

This incredible woman who helped to raise my Omi, whose mother was often not well, was also the woman who helped my grandparents escape from Austria and who smuggled out all of my grandmother's family's furniture that she could, shipping it to the United States once they left Belgium, where they had been living in hiding.

You see, through whatever means my grandfather had, he knew that Hitler was approaching. He insisted to his in-laws and my grandmother that they must all leave their home in the country and head to their home in Vienna that same evening. He gave Marianne the family's gold and asked her to bury it in the yard, hoping that one day they would return to find it. Marianne did exactly as he asked, burying the gold beneath the countryside soil.

They fled to Vienna that evening, with only the few items they could pack in the twenty or so minutes my grandfather had given them to prepare. They arrived at their second home in Vienna and drew the thick, heavy drapes closed to hide. Shortly thereafter, they heard the chanting and the marching, and as they peeked out through the smallest crevice of the curtains, they could see Hitler marching into the hotel across the street. The Nazis were here, right in the streets of their city. They knew they had to leave Vienna . . . that night.

My Opi had enough foresight to prepare for this moment. He had created fake Czechoslovakian passports for himself, my grandmother, and my great-grandparents to use to board the train to Belgium that evening. My grandfather and great-grandparents all spoke Czech, but my grandmother did not.

And so they boarded the train and found their seats. The Nazis walked through the cars of the train, speaking to the passengers and making sure that there were no Jews looking to do exactly what my family was bravely doing. They entered the train car where my family sat nervously waiting. My grandmother had been instructed to pretend to sleep. As the Nazis questioned my family about who they were and where they were headed, they wanted to speak to my grandmother as well. My grandfather boldly explained that she was pregnant and very tired from the travel. Begrudgingly, the SS officers moved on, and my family was safe . . . for the moment.

They lived in hiding for the next ten months. They hid in the basement of a friend's home in Belgium, until one day they were able to make their great escape to America, the country that would soon give them an opportunity to create a new life for themselves. They had so little, yet they were lucky enough to have each other.

And they never forgot those who helped them experience freedom. For the remainder of my grandfather's life, he sent money each year to Marianne and the family in Belgium that hid them, which was his way of letting them know that he would never forget the risks they took to allow him and my Omi to live. My family was small, yet, thankfully, my grandmother's sister and her side of the family were able to escape as well, but not to America—they landed in Australia. And while our family has always been divided across the globe, the love and unity has always been felt throughout the generations. And the rich history will always be remembered.

Now, to understand my grandmother, you must know that she was a bit of a rebel. Not the kind of girl that did "bad things" or got herself into trouble—no, not that kind of rebel—but rather an outspoken, honest, and direct woman who had no problem sharing her thoughts, ideas, and feelings with others. In a day and age when women, like children, "should be seen and not heard," my grandmother liked to be a bit edgy, pushing the envelope and being her true outspoken self. And that true self, that incredibly strong, brave, and honest woman, is the other pivotal female role model I was fortunate enough to have had guiding me through my first forty-seven years of life. I imagine her courage and bravery strengthened, consciously or not, during those months of fleeing the Nazi regime and continued to grow as she found her freedom in America.

I have to believe that when you come from much and it is all stripped away from you, your life at stake and angst your new default emotion, you are forever changed. While I didn't know the young girl who loved to break in horses and do rhythmic gymnastics in the Vienna countryside, I knew the woman who taught me about abundance, in the most unique way. My Omi showed me that an abundant life was not about the material things; rather, an abundant life is a life of good health, of a loving family surrounding you at the dinner table, and of being able to enjoy the moment and its memories—big and small.

Although my grandmother came from much, she was never spoiled. Her mother and father were down-to-earth, kind, generous, and always seeking to include others, especially those who had less, whether that was a lack of finances or family. As a little girl growing up, my Omi was never given everything she wanted. My great-grandparents saw to it that their two daughters were raised to value everything they had.

I remember my Omi telling me stories about her dollhouse. When she was a young child, she had a toy dollhouse, and every year for her birthday and for any big occasion, she was given one piece to add to it—a bed, a small dresser, or a tiny rug. She was never given everything to furnish the dollhouse all at once; the joy was parceled out and made so much more special by the excitement that came from seeing what piece would be uncovered next. This appreciation for the little things, and for not taking anything in life for granted, was a thread throughout my grandmother's life—one she wove into the tapestry of everything she taught me.

Omi was always making something out of nothing. She was a saver, keeping every extra button, wine cork, rubber band, glass jar, and piece of ribbon, knowing that, someday, each would prove itself useful in some yet-to-be-thought-of craft project she would dream up. Whether it was lacquered walnuts she would turn into jewelry or bottlecaps she would turn into Christmas decorations, my Omi was never short on ideas . . . or fun! She didn't believe in spoiling us, either, and she taught my brother and me how to find the joy in creating things from scraps—what others would have thrown away—and building masterpieces from nothing.

Because, as an eighteen-year-old immigrant girl, she was thrown into a new country with a new language and culture, my grandmother knew firsthand what it was like to feel confused and lost in this new world. Her resiliency to adapt—and to make do with whatever she had—empowered her to think about both the adventure and difficulties that came with it, that others immigrating to this new world might experience. Being both the bold woman and compassionate heart that she was, she and a few other ladies created the American Civic Association, an organization to help immigrants to the US learn valuable skills, such as how to find a job and how to get acclimated. She also spent her time at the hospital in Upstate New York, the region my family had immigrated to, in order to bring reassurance, love, and joy to those who were suffering. People—not things—were important to Omi.

When I was a child, there were always new faces around our dinner table—faces of strangers that soon became family. The widow who had no one to be with, the neighbor who was lonely and had nowhere to go for Thanksgiving, the couple who was new to Arizona and had no family or friends close by. Yes, my Omi was that kind of a heart, the kind that beats for others before herself. She enveloped people with her warmth and charm, and she was ALWAYS a lady. Dressed to the nines, adorned with the perfect amount of jewelry and a beautiful, yet natural, face of makeup (and just the right shade of orangey-red lipstick to match her skin tone), my Omi was one of the most classy, hardworking, brave, giving, confident, and gracious women this world has ever known. And her altruistic and grateful nature, in spite of the difficult cards she had been dealt at such a young age, is just one of the qualities that made her so extraordinary to me. I believe that because she had experienced all that she did in her lifetime, she had a different appreciation for it. She would repeatedly say, "Life made me this way," an idiom that I believe encapsulates her gratitude for her family, her appreciation of all that she DID have, her passionate determination to help support others who needed it, and her desire to keep us grounded in what truly matters most—never the "stuff," but rather the people we share our lives with.

My Omi's resilience and tenacity in life was exemplified right up until her story's end. At one hundred, she was still living on her own in her twenty-five-hundred-square-foot home. Although she had my father and a caregiver spending time with her each and every day, she was still managing quite beautifully on her own. When my Opi passed away at eighty-seven years of age, nearly twenty-five years prior, Omi told my father, brother, and me that she would live in that house until "we took her out." A little grim, but that decisive and determined attitude was my Omi.

Then on Halloween night of 2020, moments after her caregiver had left, Omi bent over to pick something up off the ground and she fell, breaking her hip. In the hospital, the doctor and surgeon who assessed her condition said that they couldn't believe it: she had the bones of a seventy-year-old; they were stunned that she was actually one hundred years old! The medical team was confident that she could withstand the hip surgery, and so that same evening, in the middle of the night, my dad and I waited anxiously as they performed the surgery. It was a success, and she did incredibly well. This mighty little woman had a long road ahead of her but in a matter of six months, she was back up and walking, with little assistance from a walker or caregiver, and while now in a care home, she was doing remarkably well.

It was only ten months after her first fall, however, that she fell again. And this time, though the doctors originally felt prepared for and confident about another surgery, we began to see that her body—which was now 101 years old—simply couldn't undergo that kind of intensity again. She wouldn't survive it, and we couldn't bear the thought of her going through that treacherous recovery process. And yet, even in those final days of her life before she passed, she would tell me what she would always tell me when times were tough: "Well, it could be worse!"

I have always marveled at her outlook on life, at her attitude. She was always realistic, yet never EVER one to complain or feel sorry for herself. She played the cards she was dealt in life, with love and appreciation for everything, uniquely herself and unlike anyone else I have ever met.

My grateful warrior of a grandmother taught me tenacity and resilience through her daily words and actions. Today, these principles of appreciating what you have while working toward what you want, all while using your gifts and talents to make the world a better place for others, are woven into every training I deliver. In our classes at U & Improved, we continually remind our students that there is no time to be stuck in our stories or to allow ourselves to play victim to our circumstances. It is up to each of us individually to remain forward-focused and to be the architects of our own lives, designing the businesses we are meant to have and the lives we are meant to live.

My Omi single-handedly taught me more than I could ever teach others. I only hope to be a fraction of that woman for my girls, and the world, that she was for me.

My grandparents called him *Goldkind*, or Golden Child. Yes, my father was their only child (his baby sister was stillborn, almost costing my grandmother her own life, which is another story altogether). Because of these factors, my grandparents obviously invested all of their love and energy into their one and only baby boy, their golden child, Jeffrey.

My father is one of the most talented, creative, and imaginative minds you will ever meet. From the time I was a small child, I remember the bedtime stories he would tell my brother and me, painting the most vivid images and the most riveting stories with characters that came to life in such a way that we were certain we knew them personally.

But my dad isn't just a creative storyteller; he lived his life with that same carefree, playful manner, always dreaming, always creating, always sparking magic wherever he went. He was a magician of sorts.

Growing up in a household with a father and older brother, and grandparents that I saw daily and who were an extremely important part of my life, I knew that how I saw and experienced life was unusual, quite different from the households my friends grew up in.

My dad has always been a fine artist and an interior designer, always working for himself and always working from home. It was magnificent as a child, because my dad was actively engaged in my life, there for all the milestones and memories, to a greater extent than for many of my friends who had two-parent households. At no time in my life was this more apparent than when I was in elementary school.

When I was a little girl attending Kiva Elementary School (where, you may recall, my dad met Suzanne), I was made vividly aware of just how different my dad was from all the others. Back when I was a child, our elementary school years were filled with class parties and field trips. Always the highlight of our month, these were the events that every child looked forward to, but none more than I.

While many classrooms had a "homeroom mom" or two that helped the teacher plan and organize these outside events, my grade school classroom was different. We had a "homeroom dad." And not just any dad—MY dad.

My dad would make every holiday party feel extra special. He would bring his own colored chalk and draw Rudolph with his bright red nose, Santa and his long white beard, or balloons to celebrate that month's birthdays up on the chalkboard. I remember how the other children would sit and stare in awe at how quickly and effortlessly he would create these masterpieces before their eyes, and how one little girl ran up to him and said sweetly with a big hug, "I wish you were MY daddy."

Those moments in elementary school stuck with me (and with the teachers who had to clean all that colored chalk off those dusty green boards) because they were the first times I actually realized that my home life was different from most.

But it wasn't until the Shamrock Dairy field trip that this all truly hit home for me.

It was a warm spring day in Arizona, not unlike most days in my home state. Mrs. Head's third-grade class was eagerly awaiting the morning bell's ring so that we could enter the classroom and drop off our backpacks, and then line up to board the big yellow school buses.

Field trip days were the best, an adventure waiting to happen and a sense of freedom from the mundane school routine. We kids were antsy and excited as we waited anxiously to get the party started!

The bell rang, backpacks were dropped, and the rambunctious group of seven- and eight-year-olds were told to settle down in our seats while we waited for our chaperones to arrive back from the office where they were getting all the permission slips submitted to administration.

The chaperone team walked in, ready to go. My dad waved slyly to me as he stood amid the other moms who volunteered to help that day. As they all waited in the back of the classroom for a few minutes while the teacher gathered her belongings and kept us as quiet as she could amid our excitement, I noticed how my dad stood out—both because he was the only father there, and because he always dressed sharply and had a smile across his face that could light up a room. He always brought that joy, excitement, and sense of wonderment to everything he did, and I loved that about him. He and the chaperone team looked ready for action and adventure that morning, and all of us kids were so excited to get out of the classroom and on with the field trip!

However, one little girl in our class was struggling. Kirsten was a very sweet, and very frail, young girl who was born with some kind of degenerative disease that caused her bones to not grow properly. She was extremely skinny, with legs that were so fine and thin you wondered how she could even manage to take a step. But she did take a step—several actually, much like a young fawn taking her first few wobbly steps. However, after just a few minutes, Kirsten would get very tired and would need assistance or a break.

Now, I am not sure why Kirsten didn't have a wheelchair or a walker—because that was something unavailable to her or perhaps something she preferred to do without—but it became clear to the chaperones that this day may be a bit much for her, given that there was probably going to be a lot of walking involved.

"No problem!" my dad said. "Kirsten, will you be my buddy for today?" Kirsten's little face lit up, and she nodded with a smile.

We set off to board the school buses, each of the third-grade classes boarding their own bus. As we all piled in, it was the usual chaos you would find on an elementary school field trip day: little boys pulling little girls' ponytails, giggling and talking when we were told ad nauseum to be quiet, screaming and bouncing on the school bus seats like little Mexican jumping beans (another huge '80s novelty item, by the way; if you don't know what they are, google them . . . they're awesome).

And so we ventured out of the parking lot on our long drive across town toward the Shamrock Dairy to see how milk and dairy products are made and manufactured and end up on our grocery store shelves. My dad was sitting in the very front of the bus, with his buddy for the day, Kirsten, nestled beside him.

As we began to pull out of the parking lot, the volume of the kids on the bus became so loud that the bus driver was getting upset. "Settle down, kids, or we're not going anywhere!" he shouted as he stopped the bus before we even made it out to the main road.

The class quieted down, but only for a moment. Then the cacophony of screaming and laughing began once more.

"Kids, we will NOT leave until you quiet down!" the bus driver said, his voice booming with anger.

Enter the Creative Warrior, my amazing dad.

"Kids!! Who's ready to play a game?" my dad said.

The kids perked up at once, knowing that Mr. Low always brought the fun.

"Okay, I need you to be very, very quiet as I explain the directions, because this game is a tough one!" he continued.

All eyes were fixated on my father.

"So this is how the game works. I am going to walk around the school bus and hand each of you your very own imaginary plastic spoon," he began. "Now this plastic spoon is just for you, and when I hand it to you, I am going to ask you to open your mouth, so I can place the end of the spoon handle in your mouth . . . does that make sense?"

Thirty little heads nodded in anticipation.

"Now, be very careful with your spoon. When I place the handle in your mouth, I am also going to be placing an imaginary ice cube on the opposite end of your spoon that you will need to balance, so you will need to close your lips tightly around that spoon handle so you don't drop your ice cube! Your challenge is to see who can hold their imaginary ice cube on their imaginary spoon the longest . . . are you all ready?"

"YES!!!" the kids clamored.

My dad, in his most amazing and magnetic and energetic way, ran up and down the length of that bus as we tore down the streets of Phoenix heading toward the dairy. He hurriedly handed out spoons while placing them ever so gently in each child's mouth. He balanced those imaginary ice cubes with such delicacy that no kid dared move or speak in fear of dropping either.

He rushed to wipe the imaginary water that was dripping down one girl's cheek, while placing a new spoon in the mouth of the little boy who had whispered to my dad that he had accidentally dropped his on the school bus floor. My father quickly ran down the aisle of the bus to his imaginary bag, grabbed another spoon, and whispered back, "No problem . . . here you go! We have plenty of spoons left!" And encouraged this little boy to get back in the game.

There, on that warm spring morning, thirty children sat quiet as church mice, pursing their lips tightly around their imaginary spoons while balancing their imaginary ice cubes. There, too, sat a couple of mothers in complete awe of this dad who was racing up and down the aisles of a school bus keeping thirty kids riveted with excitement and anticipation, wondering what their imaginary prize would be.

And there sat a dumbfounded school bus driver who simply said, "That man is a magician."

And he was. And he is.

In hindsight, I don't know what was more magical: that bus ride with our imaginations fully engaged or the fact that my sweet dad carried little Kirsten for two hours straight throughout the entirety of the giant dairy.

Either way, the magic never stops with my father. He continued to share this same magic and this boundless zest for creativity with my daughters, creating art projects together, playing imaginative games, and working tirelessly on school projects together, always creating literal works of art.

And now, at eighty-one years of age, one might think that his creativity may have waned a bit, that perhaps he feels a little more tired and is less apt to create. But no—not my dad. My extraordinary dad is creating some of the most beautiful art of his entire career, in my opinion, and is designing a restaurant on the East Coast, thousands of miles away. The *Goldkind*, as my grandparents so lovingly named him, continues to radiate beauty throughout the world, which I believe he feels is his moral obligation to mankind. It's who he is at his core, and I know that love of aesthetics and art and beauty in any form is what my dad seeks to share with the world.

My dad's energy, youthful spirit, and childlike ability to dream and create is something that I have admired throughout my lifetime and is one of the greatest gifts he has given me and my girls. He taught us to appreciate all the beauty around us, to activate our imaginations, and to surround ourselves with creativity whenever and wherever we can. Life is too short to live any other way. Looking back, I see how what he taught me throughout my life still shows up for me today. And I find myself passing this same energy and spirit on to my girls.

Just a few years ago, I wanted to surprise my daughters with a trip to New York City during the holidays, but rather than just telling them about it or wrapping up the airline tickets, I wanted to bring that same magic my father does and make it so much more! I wrapped up little theater marquee letters in variously sized packages to put under the tree. Each time they got an *S* or an *N*, they grew more curious (and frustrated!) about what the heck this was all about. They finally unwrapped their final letter, wondering, *Now what?* I then handed them a poster board with blank spaces on which they needed to unscramble their letters. They worked away to solve it and finally got ... not the answer, but ... *Frank Sinatra's #1 Hit*. They thought of any song they could come up with that he might have sung, but eventually turned to the almighty Google. And then, the lightbulb went off.

"New York, New York ... Wait ... wait, what? NEW YORK, NEW YORK??!?!?! Are we actually going to NEW YORK??!" they exclaimed.

"YES WE ARE!! Pack your bags, girls! We leave the day after tomorrow!" I said excitedly.

And that incredible trip, chock full of memories, was filled with the same energy and excitement my dad brought to my childhood. Each day unfolded with the magic and beauty of the experience, which we savored at every moment. And just like he taught me, I teach my girls how to create beautiful things, delight in beautiful moments, and chase after beautiful experiences whenever and wherever they can. And always, ALWAYS keep the magic alive.

———

I'm not sure how I got so lucky in the sibling department, but I am pretty sure I was a really good person in a past life, or perhaps I just happened to win the sibling jackpot. Either way, I absolutely ADORE my big brother.

Marc, or Marc-i as I call him, is six years older than I am, and while we were (and still are) the best of friends, he was always living in a different phase of life than I was growing up. Six years ahead in school and in life makes for a big age gap.

But despite that gap, my brother always included me in whatever activity he was doing or wherever he was going. We were, in fact, the best of buddies. As children, we weren't given many toys, but encouraged to appreciate and use our minds and our imaginations, which meant we were often playing board games based on strategy or doing art projects or performances using our natural talents (okay, maybe not so talented in our singing and dance moves, but we didn't care— zero inhibition). But that didn't mean that my brother didn't get me into trouble every now and then or use his "big brother cleverness" to his advantage. I remember one moment from when I was about four and he was ten: Knowing my love for chocolate, he convinced me that it was growing from the ground. I was so excited and ate some "chocolate" only to realize it was rabbit poop. He would also convince me to give him my little dimes for his big, shiny nickels, or that Milk-Bone dog treats taste just like Wheat Thins (they don't, by the way). Despite—or perhaps because of—these shenanigans, my brother and I were always playing and having fun together, no matter what.

I was only twelve years old when it came time for my brother to head off to college. I was still in middle school, and while I was so sad to see him leave for California, I knew that his dream was to head out of state to start a life of his own. My brother always loved to travel and learn and explore, so I knew he would venture out . . . someday. And someday was suddenly now.

What I didn't know at twelve years old was that this would be the last time my brother and I would ever spend together under one roof. I hadn't really thought about it in that context before that time, but the thought of him not being there to play games with me and hang out together definitely made me sad. And though he would later attend the Fashion Institute of Design & Merchandising in Los Angeles and the world-renowned Thunderbird School of Global Management in Glendale, Arizona, that was as close to "home" as he would ever live again.

After a phenomenal experience studying abroad in Munich, my brother fell in love with the heartbeat of new cultures and new experiences around the globe. So, after graduating from college, my brother decided to build his life in Europe. He worked for major global companies in the areas of marketing, merchandising, and licensing, expanding his career with opportunities that allowed him to live all over Europe.

While living abroad, he also found the love of his life, my "other brother," the most amazing Parisian man, whom I adore. I was still a teenager when they met and didn't understand their relationship at that age, until one day it dawned on me that they were a couple. And while I was sad that they didn't tell me firsthand, in hindsight I realize that back in that day and age an "alternative lifestyle" was much less accepted than it is today. I never cared. I was just so damn happy to have this amazing bonus brother in my life!

As a child, my brother was very close with our Omi. It was as if they were inseparable, and my Opi and I were the same. And while we both felt equal love from our grandparents, we both seemed to naturally gravitate toward one of them more than the other due to our common interests. My grandfather and I shared a love of language and music; he not only nurtured my love of words from the quotes he would share, but he also encouraged me to play the piano and the cello, growing my love for classical music. My brother had a natural interest in gardening and horticulture, and a love for cooking—specifically, for baking—which meant spending countless hours in the backyard and kitchen working alongside our Omi.

His connection with Omi ran so deep that he would learn a lifetime of stories through his time with her. She would share all of the details and all of the rich history of her childhood. She would share the story behind each antique and artifact in her home that Marianne had helped send over to the States. And while I sat beside my grandfather, tinkering away on the piano keys, my brother learned how to make all of the Austrian cakes and cookies, the Weiner schnitzel and the Hungarian goulash—all of our favorite dishes that our Omi would make for us.

This love of culture and cuisine, this love of seeing and understanding the world and knowing that there is so much more to our planet than sunny Arizona, is what I believe sent him on what I refer to as the journey of a lifetime. He and my Parisian brother-in-law have traveled to every continent, visiting countries I can't even locate on a map. And when they travel, they do it right. They immerse themselves in the culture and the people. They don't just see a place, they feel it. They live it. Yes, these global warriors take it all in, experiencing every inch of the world that they can.

And my "brothers" shared this way of living with me firsthand when I turned forty.

"So, we have a surprise for you," they said.

I couldn't imagine what these two had come up with. All I knew was that a surprise from them was ALWAYS good.

"We're taking you on a trip for your fortieth birthday!" they told me.

A trip!? Well, I knew a trip with these two would be nothing short of amazing, but I couldn't imagine what was ahead of me.

"Yes, we have it planned. We are going to fly you out to meet us in Paris and we'll spend a few days there before we head off to . . . Morocco!"

Morocco? As in Africa? I couldn't believe it! I was grinding it out, day after day, getting this business off the ground while doing my best to raise these two little girls and not lose my sanity in the process, and now I was going to go play in Europe and Africa with these two?! Sign. Me. UP!

To visit a country like Morocco, with two experienced world travelers, is truly the gift of a lifetime. And in a country like that, where crime is high and women are often treated as second-class citizens, I don't believe I ever would have felt safe to travel there on my own as a single woman. I knew that my brother, Marc, would appease all my fears and make this experience so much more than I ever could have imagined.

You see, Marc is the perfect combination of all of the most beautiful attributes of my family members. He has the wisdom and love of learning from my Opi, the love of family and heritage from my Omi, and the appreciation of beauty and beautiful places from my father. I knew—if Marc was planning it—this trip would be nothing short of incredible. And I was right.

I don't know if it was the snake charmers at the souks, or outdoor markets, in Marrakech or the small winding streets that led you through them, but everything about this experience was enchanting. We had dinner outside with musicians who would play their instruments sitting cross-legged on the ground while twirling the tassels atop their fez hats to the beat. I would stare, and giggle, as a server in another restaurant would pour me yet another glass of delicious mint tea from two feet above me. All these little moments are the experiences that, for me, make life worth living. The conversations we shared on this trip, about our goals and dreams, our lives as they were at the time and where we wanted them to someday be, are moments I will forever cherish.

But when I think back to this trip, what stands out the most is the lesson that my global warrior brothers have taught me:

Myopic thinking and lack of vision will get you nowhere in life. The world, and all that it has to offer, is just outside your door, and your comfort zone. All you have to do is open the door and take your first step.

Throughout my life, my brother has taught me about the vastness of the world. He has nurtured in me a love of travel. And although my life's journey didn't allow me to do and see an iota of what he has experienced, his lifestyle showed me that it's about the experiences in life—appreciating the world, its people, and all the joy there is to be found in understanding lives and cultures so different from our own.

And the most beautiful part of it all is that these two uncles are instilling this love of culture, travel, and heritage into their nieces. During one of their last visits back home to the States, my brother spent the evening making Wiener schnitzel with the girls. As he hammered each piece of veal into the finest, thinnest version of itself that he could, then carefully dipped each piece into the egg wash, flour, and breadcrumbs, my girls watched each step, jumping in to help and laughing at their giant breadcrumb-covered fingertips. We watched him lovingly prepare each little schnitzel and when it was finally time to squeeze the lemon juice on them and take our first bites, my oldest daughter proclaimed, "If I had to pick my last meal on earth, THIS would be it!" My Marc-i made that Wiener schnitzel as carefully, thoughtfully, and lovingly as our Opi did for us, and it warmed my heart . . . and my belly.

The following evening, it was time to take our taste buds to Paris. As Marc and I buzzed around the kitchen table, getting it all set and ready to eat, we smiled a coy smile at one another as we took it all in. My brother-in-law showed the girls how to make homemade French crepes, a meal he enjoyed during his childhood and throughout his time growing up in France. Making crepes is a labor of love (and a lot of work), but, wow, watching my girls stare in amazement as he flipped the crepes in the air and seeing them work right alongside him to learn the "tricks of the trade" was nothing short of delightful. And although, yes, cooking in a kitchen may seem mundane, the lessons taught in this little realm of life can linger for generations. My brother and his partner continually remind me of the importance of keeping our heritage alive and celebrating the world around us at any opportunity we can. Whether that's whisking up crepes in our kitchen in Arizona or winding along the marketplace streets of Marrakech, we can all celebrate the globe and our connections to one another, no matter how far and wide.

And as my girls and I prepare to take our first visit across the Atlantic together to visit these two in Paris, I know that my love of travel —of this great big world and all the people in it—was nurtured by the big brother that is still my best buddy and the only person who—at any moment—knows EXACTLY what I am thinking, can finish my every sentence, can challenge and rival my every play on words and best puns, and can burst into a rendition of some 1980s one-hit wonder of a song in an instant. We're connected in the most bizarre and beautiful way, and our relationship is one of the gifts in life that I am most grateful for.

Dear U,

As far as I know, we are given one shot at this thing called life. My constant question to myself is *Am I living my BEST life, and what can I do more of, differently, or better to make it so?* However, that question always leads me back inward, to my source, where I take inventory of all that I DO have, all that I am so appreciative of, while I work to grow myself and those areas of my life I wish to expand.

So my question for U is this:

What is the dream for YOUR life? Where are U, and where do U want to be?

And if U are reading these words and thinking to yourself *I am already exactly where I want to be*, then celebrate that. And keep doing more of it.

For those of U still looking, searching and yearning for more, whatever *more* means to U—more love, more joy, more health, more success, more fun, more friends, more adventures—I must also ask U this:

If not now, WHEN?

With every second, we age and get closer to the fate we will all eventually succumb to. I know this sounds morbid, being one step closer to death, but to me, it's actually an invitation to experience the world differently, to take note of your life and see what else is possible for U and those U love. Time slips by so fast, and with it, our lives.

So I invite U to learn from the wise warriors in my life, the mentors who unknowingly shaped me into the woman, mother, businessperson, trainer, and coach I am today. They instilled in me a foundation, a source that points me back to what I have that I can appreciate now and what I want to seek more of in my life.

Continually ask yourself what kind of warrior U want to focus more on becoming:

The Passionate Warrior: What am I most passionate about in life? How and where can I create even MORE passion in my life?

The Grateful Warrior: What am I most grateful for? Have I taken time recently to share my love, appreciation, and gratitude with those people and places that matter most to me?

The Creative Warrior: How do I let my creativity and magic shine? Where and how can I best let my imagination run wild and free to think new thoughts and create new things in my world?

The Global Warrior: How do I experience more of what this world has to offer me? How do I better relate to and understand those who are different from me, so that I can grow as a human being?

Or maybe there's some kind of warrior that hasn't been mentioned here but is yearning to break out and come alive within U.

Listen, these are deep questions to reflect upon, I know. But, dear reader, they are the basis of LIFE! When the sand runs out and the curtain closes, these are the things that will matter the most, and they will be both the memories U keep and the legacy U leave behind.

So don't just skim the surface. **Don't just think the easy thoughts or simply drive down the well-paved superhighways of your mind. Take the dusty country road and see where it takes U . . . see what kind of warrior U become along the way.** The new ideas, the deeper level of passion and appreciation, and the ability to see and feel the world in a whole new way will be the true gifts of your lifetime. Guaranteed.

With love and gratitude,

the
Samurai

———

CHAPTER EIGHT

The Third Child

Everybody can be great, because everybody can serve. You don't have to have a college degree to serve. You don't have to make your subject and your verb agree to serve . . . you only need a heart full of grace, a soul generated by love.
—Martin Luther King Jr.—

I always knew I wanted at least two children, and in the early days, Mike and I had sincerely entertained and discussed the idea of having three. I knew it would be a lot of work, but I always thought we could handle it between the two of us. Plus, we made some pretty cute kiddos together.

But when my life imploded back on that fateful day in October of 2008, it quickly became apparent that the dream of possibly having that third baby would never become reality. I wondered, in those early post-divorce days, what it would have been like to have had a third child. Would it have been another amazing little girl? Or a little boy this go-around? What would it be like for my girls to both be big sisters? What would our home look and feel like with a third little baby to love?

And then my daydreaming would sometimes lead to a little sadness. That chapter was closed. I was already well into my midthirties, so the clock was ticking for my body, and having a third baby clearly wasn't going to happen with Mike. Yet, as the months and years went on, I realized just how perfect it was, just me and my two little girls. My life felt full, and crazy. I had my girls and my little company that was starting to emerge—this was everything I needed and wanted.

For several years after our divorce, the girls and I lived in a home we rented from dear friends of mine who just happened to have a house coming up for rent in a perfect neighborhood right by a terrific elementary school, in a wonderful area filled with children and bustling with activity. Living in a city like Scottsdale, Arizona, where the weather is beautiful so much of the year, the sidewalks are always filled with families going on bike rides, and dogs are panting with excitement as they walk alongside their owners and enjoy the very best part of their day, and cul-de-sacs are filled with children laughing and playing . . . it was just as childhood should be.

But as the years went on, life began to change. My training team and I were delivering more and more classes, and my client list encompassed everything from small, locally owned businesses to Fortune 100 companies. My dad, who was in his early seventies at the time, was still living in Scottsdale, about twenty minutes south of us, in the home my brother and I grew up in. It was a beautiful house in the absolute heart of Scottsdale. It definitely needed a lot of updates, as it was built in the late 1970s and had only had a kitchen remodel done a few years prior, due to a flood. But my dad was done with it. He was a single man in a large house and didn't want to put the time and money into fixing it. He told my brother and me that he thought it was best to sell the house and downsize into something much smaller and more manageable. My brother and I were sad, but we understood. It was a lot of house for just him to manage, and it certainly needed some love to make it more modern.

The next time my brother happened to be in town visiting from Europe, we pulled up to the house and there it was: the *For Sale* sign planted in the front yard of our childhood home. It sucked. There were so many beautiful memories we shared within those walls, with our neighboring bedrooms and the extra little bedroom suite my dad had added when the house was first built so that my Omi and Opi could live there while their house was constructed. The pool that we spent every single summer day in, entertaining ourselves for hours on end. The family room floor where we would play countless games, me so little and just wanting ONCE to finally beat my big brother at SOMETHING.

We both looked at each other.

"It's so sad," my brother said. "Somehow, I just thought we'd always have this house."

"Yeah, me too. I can't believe someone else will actually be living here soon. It just doesn't feel right," I added.

A pause.

"Jodi, what if there was a way YOU could buy the house from dad and you and the girls could live here?" my brother exclaimed, the idea just hitting him as he spoke the words out loud.

"Well, that would be amazing but I am putting every dime into the business and the girls, and there's been zero child support from Mike anymore . . ."

"Dad is helping you out with the girls quite a bit, picking them up from school when you have meetings, feeding them dinner and putting them to bed if you have a weekend training. What if you could all live together?" he said excitedly.

"All live . . . together?" I added, less than enthused. I had just come to a point in this new version of my life's story where I was a single mother raising my girls and feeling really good about where we were headed. The idea of another person living with us seemed almost foreign to me now. I was so accustomed to it just being our little trio. Would my dad be overwhelmed with having the girls around so much? Would we all feel crowded and get a bit sick of each other if we were together EVERY day?

"Think about it. Dad could sell you the house, but instead of having to make the down payment, you could just take over the mortgage. Slowly, over time, you can remodel portions of the house and make it look how you want it to, but for now, it's certainly more than fine how it is. In return, he could move into the extra suite and be separate from you and the girls, so you all have your own space, but he would be there to help you out and, in exchange, he would have no mortgage or lease to pay. What do you think? It's a way to keep the house in the family, give you and the girls a home of your own again, get Dad out from having to manage a big house on his own, give you the extra help you need, give the girls another family member outside of only you to build a tight bond with, and lower his expenses so he doesn't have to worry about working too hard and can enjoy himself more and spend more time with the girls!" he went on.

I thought about it. But not for long. Leave it to my big brother—this was a brilliant idea! A home of our own, yet the ability for the girls to have a father figure in their life each day. And my dad and I get along so well. "MARC!" I exclaimed. "This is such a great thought! Do you think Dad will go for it?"

He did go for it. Not only did he go for it, he was over the moon. As you all may remember, my dad is an easygoing, up-for-anything kind of a guy, so this next adventure sounded great to him! His eyes lit up at the idea and he was all in! Seeking out those win-win situations in the spirit of my U the Communicator courses, I was all about seizing this win-win-win experience, for my dad, for the girls, and for me.

And so we began cleaning and sorting, both his house and ours. Years of papers and artwork and paints and colored paper at my dad's house, and plastic pieces of birthday party favors and leotards and stuffed animals at our house. But I was ready. This was a job, all right, but I was ready to roll up my sleeves and begin this next chapter of my life with my little girls and my favorite magic-maker by my side.

I had no idea that this next chapter would give me a third child.

No, no, this wasn't a human child. This was a completely different kind of a birth . . . and a completely different kind of child. But just like my other two, this one was also a gift from above.

————

This particular story started on a cold and rainy weekend up in the cool pines of Prescott, Arizona. My incredible training team, assistants, and I were up in northern Arizona for one of our favorite classes to facilitate, U the Warrior. U the Warrior is an advanced two-and-a-half-day leadership training course that we teach at U & Improved, and while the first night of the course takes place at our hotel facility in Scottsdale, the following morning of class happens in the small town of Prescott, Arizona. Our trainers and students all drive a couple of hours north and meet outside of the classroom, and we spend much of our time in the great outdoors.

Each of our leadership training courses at U & Improved focuses on various leadership (and life) competencies. And for this particular class, the overarching theme is to answer the question *What is the dream for your life?* All of the experiential processes and activities revolve around uncovering the answer to this question, allowing participants to deeply challenge themselves to look internally, and to their fellow classmates, to find their own answers to that highly involved question.

It was on the second day of this three-day class that we all headed up north, and unlike years prior, this morning on the drive up, we could see some ominous dark clouds hanging in the sky above us. This had us concerned because several of the outdoor elements we incorporate in the class involve metal cables and wires, not things anyone can be on or near were a lightning storm to occur.

The morning started out cool and overcast, but as the day progressed, those clouds grew thicker and darker, and as we checked the weather report every few minutes, we could see that there was no lightning in the forecast, only heavy rains. We were relieved, but any outdoor processes in the rain were going to add an extra degree of difficulty, and we knew that the amazing warriors-to-be in this class would handle some rain just fine. So we donned our plastic ponchos and kept going as the rain began to fall.

Although I don't want to give too much away ('cause I am a big dreamer and, who knows, maybe one day, you, dear reader, will join us in class?!), what I will say is that our students were amazing at this particular outdoor experience. They were pushing themselves, challenging each other, and becoming an incredible team (or tribe, as we refer to them in this class) before my eyes. As always, it was magic happening in real time.

As the relentless rain poured down and the training team and I chuckled about the sheer volume of rain we were experiencing, I had a deep sense of "knowing" come over me. Now, I am not some super woo-woo metaphysical junkie by any means; however, I do believe we are given certain signs and inclinations in life. As I shared with you earlier in this book, whenever I feel that something is just right for me, or "true" to me, I'll instantly be covered in goose bumps. So call it whatever you like: divine intervention, spirit, the universe . . . whatever it is or was, as I stood there in my green plastic poncho, looking like a drowned rat, I had a *feeling*. And yet, this feeling was unlike anything I had ever experienced before. As you might recall, I have had some weird and woo-woo moments before, like when I had those bizarre feelings about Mandy being pregnant or when even my little daughter Alex just knew I was hurting inside and toddled off to get me a tissue when my heart was breaking. But this? This was different. It was as though I wasn't even in control of the words as they tumbled from my lips; I was simply sharing the download that was placed in my mind. It was a completely different sense of "gut feeling," unique to this moment and completely foreign to me. And yet IN the moment, during all of this, I didn't stop or pause to think about any of it. No moments of contemplation or questioning—just sharing what I knew needed to be shared.

I leaned over to Dean, one of our master trainers at U & Improved, and said, "There's a fourth class that needs to be written. Are you up for helping me write it?"

Now, mind you, I had no idea what was happening. Much as the rain was falling out of the sky, the words were spilling out of my lips before I could stop and catch them.

"Ummm, sure??" Dean said, a bit puzzled and confused. "You want to create ANOTHER class?" he said, with a bit of questioning in his voice.

I knew where the questioning and hesitancy was coming from. U the Warrior was always the pinnacle: the advanced-level leadership class that pushed every boundary, shattered every comfort zone. Even now, as we watched our warriors battling the elements to become a better "U" for themselves, I knew he was thinking to himself, *How could we possibly top this?*

And under any other circumstance, I might have been asking myself that same question. But like I said, this was a completely new sense of "knowing" and I just knew, and even said aloud to him, "This isn't about topping anything. It's not that we have to make this class 'EVEN BIGGER AND BETTER' than U the Warrior. This is something completely different. This is simply the next level . . ."

There was a fourth class that needed to be birthed. I just knew it.

The day carried on, and our soggy, yet fierce, warriors battled through the elements, finding their strength (and themselves) in the process. I watched them push themselves, and each other, and thought to myself how life changing this class really is. During the quiet moments, as we walked from one area of the beautiful and serene property to the next, my mind kept generating ideas for this new course, and I talked with our incredible training team, bouncing thoughts and ideas between each other like a Ping-Pong match. What would it be about? What wisdom would it impart? Why was it so important?

As we walked and talked, and talked and walked, over the next day, we even began sorting through names for what this next new class would be called. As when choosing a name for a child, it had to be that perfect fit—a name that would illuminate its true essence to anyone that heard it. But this wasn't a child we were looking to birth. This was some kind of an "experience"—a class with processes and activities and concepts and a journey that we hadn't even begun to formulate. I didn't know what ideas and lessons we were looking to convey yet; it was all just a tiny seed of a thought that had been planted in my mind. And then Dean whispered a name that came to him, and I instantly knew: THAT was it.

The magic that is U the Warrior continued to unfold throughout the final day, and, as usual, we remained engrossed in watching each warrior defy their own limiting beliefs and push themselves beyond anything they had ever thought possible. The class concluded with the powerful and intimate graduation celebration that is always the special bow that tops off this experience.

At each of our graduations, every student has an opportunity to share a little about their experience and address anyone there they would like to thank, or simply say something to, from their heart. The words are, without exception, so pure and raw; it's a moment I love and look forward to each and every class.

This moment now arrived for our Warriors who were graduating that day. One of my dearest friends, our insanely talented lead trainer for U the Warrior, Deno, was telling the alumni and guests in the audience about the weekend, about the graduates, and about the powerful obstacles they overcame, both literally and figuratively.

From there, Deno invited me up to speak and conclude the graduation ceremony, as usual. Deno has a special way of introducing me that somehow always seems to make me teary-eyed before I even walk to the front of the room to speak. There is a kindness and honesty, and, most importantly, a sincerity and love, in his words that is the epitome of both him and our entire training team—the authenticity that is truly the heartbeat of U & Improved. As I walked up, wiping the corners of my eyes with the tissue I KNEW to bring up with me, I began to tell everyone about what I witnessed throughout the weekend: the growth, the courage, the fortitude, and the resilience. And as I shared these thoughts with the crowd, words began spilling . . . again.

"I have some INCREDIBLY exciting news to share with you all here today!" I said, in a bit of wonderment myself, mirroring the look I saw in the faces of my training team. "U the SAMURAI is coming next spring!"

And there it was. Out in the universe.

"Deno, Dean, and I, and our training team, will be bringing this course to life over the next year, and we are so excited to share it with you next spring!"

In truth, we were just as excited to share it with ourselves because we didn't have a word of content written or any idea where we were headed. But it didn't matter. I just knew.

The room was abuzz. The energy was palpable and the pure excitement was real.

"Oh my gosh . . . YES!" someone said.

"I can't WAIT!" said another.

"What could we possibly do that we haven't already done in these first three classes?! BRING IT!!!" said a third.

As the graduation concluded and we loaded our cars with all of our training gear and supplies, I jumped into my car excited and exhausted—the same feelings I have after every U & Improved class draws to a close.

It was just Dean and me on that drive back to Phoenix. While I sat in the passenger seat and he drove, we began to make our way out of our training facility site and back onto the main roads of Prescott.

Suddenly, it all just hit me.

"WHAT THE HELL DID I JUST DO?!" I said to him in shock.

It was as though leaving the cool pines of the retreat center and reentering the "real world" snapped me back into reality and out of the ethereal heart space I had been ruminating in over the past few days.

"WHAT THE HELL IS U THE SAMURAI?" I said, now almost laughing.

And then, the kindest words . . .

"You did what you always do, Jodi. You said what you felt, and now you'll make it happen," Dean said.

Boom. There it was. Conception. Just like the tap on the shoulder from Les Brown so many years prior, Dean's words gave me that one thing I needed to secure my knowing: true belief. The seed was real and it was time to fertilize it, water it, and nurture it.

———

The next months were a whirlwind of activity. Besides being ever present for my now six- and eight-year-old daughters, growing and filling our classes, and expanding our training curriculum, I was committed to bringing this new class to life. And on top of it all, I was in the midst of cleaning out thirty-five years of stuff my dad had held on to. It was a lot, and he wasn't able to help much, so if it was gonna be, it was up to me.

During those next few months, Dean and Deno would fly in from Las Vegas and Reno, where they lived, respectively (yes, "Deno from Reno"), to help me conceptualize and create this new class. And Tiffany, my beautiful soul sister, was right there with us, ready to contribute, like always.

The four of us would meet for a few days at a time. We would reserve the conference room in our office building and hole up in there for hours and hours, only breaking for restroom runs, coffee refills, and a quick meal here and there, although we typically ordered in to make the best use of every valuable second together.

U the Samurai . . .

Our first entry point into understanding how to make this class come to life was simply to ask ourselves, *What was a true samurai warrior back in history and in Japanese culture?*

We researched and we read. We googled and we brainstormed. The whiteboard would be full of black ink and then we would photograph it, so as not to lose a single idea, and we would start all over again. We drew charts and arrows, one idea spawning the next and yet another. Tiffany would type away on her laptop as ideas upon ideas would spill from all four of us, and she would capture them all and create a to-do list to accompany every brainstorm.

And as we dove deeper and deeper into our research it all began to lie itself out before our eyes.

Bushido.

The "way of the warrior."

Bushido was the code of honor, the moral compass, developed by Japanese samurai that includes the attitudes, behavior, lifestyle, and code of ethics by which one should live. THIS was it. This is what I felt and knew, back in the cool pines of northern Arizona, needed to be brought to the world in a modern, relatable way.

Bushido consists of eight attributes, including honor, courage, compassion, and integrity, by which a human being should live their life. These eight attributes became our guideposts.

We began to take one another's ideas and push them further. As we sat around that conference room table, we continually asked one another, "What if?" What if each student, each samurai warrior in the making, were to EARN each virtue of Bushido? What if they were challenged to think and act differently, more differently than they ever had in their lives, and by partaking in a heartfelt act of courage, or compassion, or integrity, they each earned a symbolic takeaway to remind them of what they achieved? And what if, throughout this two-and-a-half-day course, they were taken so far outside their comfort zone—put into real-life scenarios that were so moving, so soul-searching, so deep—that there would be no possible way to look at humanity and the world in the same way ever again?

I remember the anticipation in the weeks leading up to the moment we would launch the very first U the Samurai class. I remember the laughs and excitement, the *Oh my gosh, could we really do THAT?* moments as we put all of the pieces of each process together. But what I didn't realize as we all sat around that conference room table for days on end each month was exactly what we were creating. I couldn't have known its magnitude, much like a first-time parent can never adequately know the immense, immeasurable, and immediate love they can feel for a tiny human being they have brought into the world until they hold that baby for the very first time.

When launch day finally arrived on that warm spring day, we reflected back on all the time and love and energy it took to design this beautiful class, and we realized it took us exactly nine months to create it—just like a child.

This was my third child. The third child I never had.

That day, we stood ready with bellies filled with butterflies, feeling as if we were sharing our new baby with the world for the very first time. Would they love it as much as we did? Would they find it as beautiful as we thought it was? They would. We knew they would.

And yet, nothing could have prepared me for the feeling I had when I saw the students, our first tribe of future samurai warriors, walk into the hotel lobby. They trusted us. They trusted us so much. They had each been through all three of our challenging, rigorous, and life-altering courses, but they had no idea of the journey they were about to embark upon. And while they had the nervous butterflies too, wondering what we could possibly have created this time, they were ready.

I even heard a student say, "If there are alligators involved, I might have to tap out! But nah, never mind . . . bring on the gators!" I knew he was joking and yet I knew exactly what he was saying. I had to laugh and smile and hold back the tears of excitement and the tears of gratitude for that level of trust. They knew they were safe and in the hands of a team of trainers that were so much more than that. We were, and are, a family. And the bond and ties in this family run deep.

Now, I would love to share with you each and every process, each heartstring-pulling experience that forever shapes and reshapes the minds and hearts of our students. Alas, I can't do that, because there is a special, almost sacred, feeling to this class. We always tell our graduates that there are no secrets in our classes—share every thought, feeling, takeaway, benefit, and lesson you learned with anyone and everyone! That's one of the most beautiful ways to give to others and to anchor in the learning for yourself. However, U the Samurai has some experiences embedded in it that defy words. So much so that we have no great marketing materials or explanations for this class that we can share on our website. The best we can do or say is, "Please just trust us and experience it for yourself."

And ever since we birthed this class into the world, that's all we've done: trust the process. And that's what our graduates do too. And it continues to happen: people step into this process full of trust, and when they step out as a samurai, this beautiful heart-shaped ripple happens where a pebble is cast into the proverbial water and that love ripples from one human being to the next. And through the power of learning about leadership, each person looks at the world through the lens of love.

As it turns out, we created exactly what we set out to create around that conference room table. A class full of transformative, immersive moments that pushed each and every student—and trainer—to look at the world differently. And I know this because these are the kinds of words shared with me, without exception, by Samurai graduates after each and every class:

"I will never look at my life, or humanity, the same way ever again . . ."

"It's as though you took my heart out of my body, massaged it, and put it back in . . ."

"I have a degree of empathy now that I never knew or felt or experienced prior to this . . . in my entire LIFETIME. I am forever changed for the better because of this class."

What's most important about these graduates' words is that they aren't just words that I hear after the rush and "high" of a powerful weekend immersion course; I SEE it in their actions. They put the learning into purposeful action, and that, to me, is the TRUE, tangible impact.

Beyond the virtues of the samurai warrior that our students learn and experience in the class, as part of the experience, I also task them with a challenge upon graduating. One of my core beliefs is that the learning in any of our classes must be actionable and sustainable. I want to be sure that our graduates apply what they learn immediately so that it sticks and becomes a part of them rather than just occasionally remembering "that great and powerful class I took a few years back." I want to keep the learning alive. I want it to be a defining moment in their lives. So at the end of the class, I hand each new samurai warrior a black polished stone with a silver infinity symbol hand-painted on it. I ask them to remember what they learned and experienced over the past few days, how it shaped them and how it changed them, and I ask them to find some way, unique and special to them, to pay it forward to someone else—some act of kindness or way of giving to someone or something else. But the key is *it must be anonymous*. This isn't about us; it's about giving back to the world, without gain or glory—just pure giving from the heart.

And it's amazing to see the giving hearts of our samurai graduates in action. That has been one of the greatest gifts for me and our training team: seeing these incredible human beings continually pouring themselves—their time, their money, their energy, and their love—into the community and other people. It's nothing short of awe-inspiring to see the Christmas tree in the hotel ballroom where we train our classes flooded with toys to be donated to a grassroots organization serving children battling rare, life-threatening illnesses or see graduates simply handing me an envelope and saying, "Jodi, please anonymously gift a seat in the next U the Samurai class to someone you know deserves it . . . I want to pay this experience forward." Others do it quietly and discreetly, in their own special way, unique and meaningful to them, and we never hear about it. But we feel it. And we see it in their eyes. Ah, giving from the heart with no expectation of getting anything in return. This is the deep joy that fills my heart and is my reason for being.

So when people ask me, "What are you most proud of in your career?" U the Samurai is it. And it's not me I am proud of. Oh no. Because U the Samurai wasn't "me"; it didn't come from me. U the Samurai came *through* me, and it only came to life and exists today because of the handful of amazing hearts that sat around that conference room table with me, simply seeking to improve the world.

We created this course to dive deep into people's hearts, and I couldn't help but reflect on the three hearts I came home to that evening after my drive back from Prescott after our U the Warrior graduation. There, in our new home—a home that was new to us as three generations under one roof together—I couldn't help but realize that, just like that infinity symbol, this chapter of our new life was all in perfect harmony. My children were now living in the bedrooms that formerly belonged to my brother and me, I was living in what was once my father's bedroom, and my dad was now living in the suite that used to house my grandparents. It was a perfect circle. I was raising my two daughters as a single parent, with the love and support of my girls' only living grandparent, just as my brother and I were raised with the love of my dad and my Omi and Opi. The love flowed through the home again just as it had when I was a child. And new memories were ready to be made together as this next cycle of our life was beginning to unfold.

It flowed.

It was *right*.

And I, too, got to feel what it's like to simply trust the process.

Dear U,

Remember when I shared a favorite quote of mine by Winston Churchill earlier in this book? "To each there comes in their lifetime a special moment when they are figuratively tapped on the shoulder and offered the chance to do a very special thing, unique to them and fitted to their talents. What a tragedy if that moment finds them unprepared or unqualified for that which could have been their finest hour." U may recall that when I shared this quote, I referred to the literal tap on the shoulder I received from Mr. Les Brown way back when I was just getting my sea legs under me after my divorce. But what if the *literal* tap never comes? What if it comes as less of a tap and more of a whisper?

As someone who has been fortunate enough to experience both, let me offer U the best advice I can:

Pay attention.

Pay attention to the people U meet, the words U hear, the invitations U get, the ideas U have, the dreams U dream—pay attention to it all. Sometimes, it's a loud, thunderous roar that wakes U from a dead sleep. Other times, it's like a woodpecker, slowly and steadily carving its indelible mark. Still, other times, it's a whisper so faint U have to strain to hear it. But however it comes to U, U must open up not only your ears but, most importantly, your heart and your gut. That's your knowing, your intuition, that sense of feeling something so strongly that it's unquestionable to U.

And while this comes easily to some, others must work on it and nurture it along so that they can become more aware. Others will never tap into it and just ask those in their sphere of influence what they should do, how they should live—and then wonder why they didn't go after their dreams or get further ahead in their lives.

If U are looking for ways to tap into that gut of yours, that sense of "knowing," I would encourage U to begin by really taking the time to get to know yourself. I mean REALLY get to know U!

Find a quiet space, grab a journal or a notepad and your favorite beverage, and ask yourself the following important questions:

1. **What matters to me?**
2. **What drives me?**

3. What gets me excited in life?
4. What people or things in life get me up early and keep me up late?
5. Why am I here?

Yes, I know . . . deep and big and rich questions. And that's exactly the point.

Do U want to continue to live life without a GPS system, without a North Star, and just end up wherever life takes U? Or would U prefer to live the balance of your years being conscious and aware, listening to your gut instinct, being in pursuit of what truly matters to U, and surrounding yourself with what truly brings U joy?

It's all a choice, dear reader. **Your gut can whisper and it can roar.** But the message of the lion is no more powerful than that of the songbird; they are simply different.

So if U find yourself at a crossroads, wondering what is next for U, what is the right path, what U should do next, I humbly invite U to be still. Be quiet. And simply . . . listen.

With love and gratitude,

CHAPTER NINE

Infinity and Beyond

*The two most important days in your life are the day you are born
and the day you find out why.*
—Mark Twain—

I never even considered having four children. For me, two or three always seemed like the sweet spot. Someone once told me when I was a young mother considering whether I would like to have more than two children, "Just remember, Jodi, one is one, two is two, and three is seven!" And that stuck. So the idea of a fourth . . . no way. Not even a consideration.

But what I have noticed throughout my fifty years on this planet is this: sometimes the most beautiful gifts come when you least expect them. And this happened for me shortly after my third child, my samurai warrior class, was born.

At this point, U & Improved, as a company, was celebrating its seventh birthday. And if you are an entrepreneur or know much about start-ups, you know that hitting the five year mark in a business is a major milestone to celebrate. The vast majority of businesses fail within the first five years of launching, whether due to lack of capital or funding, lack of clientele, or a product or service that simply doesn't take off. Entrepreneurship is not for the faint of heart. It's blood, sweat, and tears, 24-7. It's no joke. Knowing this, to be in our seventh year of business was a really exciting time. U the Samurai had just become a part of our suite of classes and momentum and notoriety for the work we do was growing. The tipping point was happening.

But something was going on in my mind. There was an ever-present knocking at the door of my mind that I couldn't ignore. It began as a soft little tap, something that I shrugged off because life was so busy. But over several years, it became an all-out banging of fists, too loud for me to ignore, and it was time to answer the call.

For the past seven years, since we began delivering our intense two-and-a-half-day classes on a regular basis, I would have graduates approach me on the day of their graduation, or after they had gone back to their homes and businesses and lives, to share something very profound with me.

"Jodi, these classes have changed my life! I can't imagine what my life would look like had I done this sooner!"

"This experience has been life changing! There are so many things that I wish I would have known when I was younger . . . I wish I would have understood life this way when I was a young adult, but I am so grateful to have these skills and tools now!"

The faces and voices would change, but the themes would remain the same. "You and your classes have changed my life" and "I wish I had this when I was younger" were the messages I was hearing over and over again. And as that pounding message got louder and more and more people continued to come up and share it with me, I simply couldn't ignore it.

Now let me backtrack for a quick minute on this concept of "You changed my life" or "Your classes are life changing." If you know me and our training team at U & Improved, the training is NEVER—and I repeat, NEVER—about us. And the day it does become about us is the day I close it all down. U matter most. Period.

The truth was it was very difficult for me to hear the beautiful intention behind "You changed my life," especially in the early years of starting the company. I wasn't prepared for the kudos or the responsibility. So I often had to sit with it for a bit and dissect it. What I recognized through my processing was that when I hear those words, I have to reframe them. I acknowledge and appreciate the compliment with a sincere and heartfelt "Thank U" and then explain that I am not the one who changed their life. THEY have made the conscious choice and decision to make those changes and improvements, to use the tools they have been given. The trainers and I have simply given them the framework and the platform to do so. We open the door; they have to choose to walk through it.

Ownership and accountability for their strength and courage in doing the hard work in their lives and businesses is important for each student to recognize, and it's equally important to me that they realize that we appreciate the compliments so very much, AND the choice is still completely theirs and theirs alone. So when graduation comes around, I'm always celebrating that fact: *U changed your life! U did it!*

And now for that second part of the call: "I wish I had this when I was younger." This intrigued me and made me pause and consider a different path that U & Improved had yet to take.

As usual, I gathered up my amazing training team, then I asked the question.

"Guys, what do you think of creating a leadership class for teenagers?!"

Now, this suggestion wasn't met with the same "What the hell is she talking about?!" look I got when I suggested the idea of U the Samurai.

They all knew it too. They, as much as or even more than me, could hear and see and feel the shifts and changes and improvements our graduates would speak about. They would hear the very same call, "If only I had this sooner . . ." and "I wish I knew this when I was younger . . ."

This time, they all just nodded and said, "LET'S DO IT!"

Our team of trainers is so talented and has so many decades of experience—their talent is unparalleled. And many of them had done leadership development work with teenagers in the past, so we sat down and got to work, believing in our expertise, our past experiences with youth, and our ability to make something magical with the tools we'd picked up along the way. The great part about this process was that it came together very quickly. We already had our proven and powerful U the Leader leadership class to create it from; we simply needed to dissect the class, section by section, and add and adjust and tweak it to make it the perfect fit for high school students.

Or so I thought . . .

It wasn't quite so easy. There was a lot to do. A LOT to dissect, and tweak, and create.

Teenagers are in a completely different stage of life and development. Their worries and doubts, their dreams and aspirations, their limiting beliefs and self-talk, while similar to adults, are still vastly different due to their lack of life experience. They simply haven't had the time and the years to truly step into life like most adults have.

So once again, we took to the drawing board, or in our case, the good old conference room, and got to work.

And again, despite all the dissecting and tweaking, it flowed. The process of creating this course unfolded so naturally. We spent time talking to teens and researching more and more about life as a teen today, versus when WE were their age. We wanted, and NEEDED, to see life through their eyes, not simply through our memories. A lot had changed, and we wanted to be sure this training was relevant, and real, and landed squarely with them. So as the Expo marker hit that whiteboard yet again, that was our focus.

Given that a few of us on the training team had kids that were approaching high school age or in high school already, we were very aware of a lot of the new pressures and threats that kids of this generation were facing. One of these pressures was simply the speed at which they can obtain information via the internet and can share it through social media—the reality that everything they do or say can be captured and exposed to the world in an instant, memorialized forever. The ways and means of accessing anything they want to know or get their hands on through hidden social media accounts, and the insane pace at which it all changes so things cannot be easily tracked, was also not lost on us. Our course needed to be relevant to these pressures of living in a rapidly evolving digital world. And on top of it all, we needed to understand the trials and tribulations, the fears and worries, the doubts and despair, and also all of the wonderful things that this stage of life can bring: the hope and excitement for what their future holds; the ideas and creativity they have for things that we, the generations before them, have never dreamed of; and the desire to go out and make a significant and lasting impact in the world.

As our next adult U the Leader class came upon us, it was time for me to share this exciting new course, to let our graduates know what we had been working on behind the scenes and what we were so excited to bring forth in a few months.

As the weekend-long adult class was drawing to a close and our alumni began to flood into the hotel to cheer on our newest graduates at their graduation celebration, it felt, yet again, like I was about to shout out and share the big "SURPRISE" that gets a whole room excited and ready to party!

The graduation ceremony began and all of our graduates received their diplomas with the universal sense of accomplishment and pride that makes onlookers' hearts soar. They had just completed a rigorous course that took them on the longest eighteen-inch journey—from their head to their heart—and they were forever changed, in a positive way, because of it. Seeing the passion, conviction, and sheer joy on their faces is a feeling that never gets old for me and is truly why I do what I do. As the graduates then shared with the audience of family, friends, and coworkers about their experience and what benefits they received from the weekend, I stood in the back of the room listening to each of them, as I always did, with a sense of knowing that today was going to be a great day, and a BIG day, as we took our own next step in helping shape future generations of leaders.

The graduation was drawing to a close and Dean, who marvelously and passionately led this team all weekend, shared some closing thoughts before introducing me and bringing me up to the front of the room. As the applause began and I quickly walked to the front of the room, I felt that intense excitement brewing. I was finally able to share the big news!

As I stood there in front of the ballroom full of smiling and exhilarated faces, I began by congratulating our most recent graduates and thanking all of the guests who were there to support them, not just that afternoon at their graduation, but every day, in their lives outside of those hotel room walls. I shared a bit about my passion for why we love what we GET to do each day and how impacting people's lives in a positive way is my mission in life and the legacy I hope to one day leave behind.

And then, drawing from the virtues of a true samurai, ready to love and serve the world, I shared with the audience the importance of the ripple effect: how each life we interact with, through the words we share and the way we show up, has a compound effect, good or bad. And I spoke about how our impact, generationally, shapes the future; the way we talk to and treat the next generation of young people has a direct influence and impact on how they lead and love throughout their own lives.

"Over the past eight or so years, adults have graduated from our classes and told me repeatedly how they only wish they would have had these skills and tools when they were younger, how they would have made different choices and decisions had they been more confident, more self-aware, had they had more self-esteem and been able to use their voice and speak their ideas with conviction," I shared with the audience.

"Well, I have heard you. And it's time to do something about it, to make sure that we help change the narrative for future generations. It's time that we give young people tools that many, and most people, never received. Today, I have news to share with you that has all of us at U & Improved so excited! This August, we will be launching a brand-new class, just for high school students aged fourteen to eighteen, called U the TEEN Leader!" I exclaimed.

And the crowd . . . went . . . wild.

Literal cheers and people jumping from their seats. They were THAT excited that we now had a means of reaching kids at that pivotal age and could truly make an impact that would forever change the trajectory of their lives.

As they smiled and whistled, I saw out of the corner of my eye a gentleman I knew well stand up from his seat, as if to speak. He was a huge-hearted guy who was also an extremely talented massage therapist—someone I had known for years and who had a passion for giving back and helping others.

"Jodi, excuse the interruption . . . I would like to sponsor a teenager."

What?? I thought to myself. *Sponsor a teenager??*

Before I could collect my thoughts about what he just said, an attorney who had recently graduated from our classes then stood up. As she popped up from her chair, she excitedly said, "Jodi, my firm would like to sponsor a teen as well!" And then, a third person jumped from their chair to say the same thing.

I was floored. I had no words. All I could feel were the tears as they slid down my cheeks and the absolute shock as I stood there baffled by what was happening.

"What??" I now said aloud. "You all want to sponsor teens through this class? REALLY?? I . . . I'm at a loss for words . . ." I said as the tears of pure joy continued to fall.

And that was the pivotal *a-ha* moment, right there in the hotel ballroom filled with our amazing graduates. There was something here even bigger than I had ever imagined. The stone had been cast into the pond. This was the first step in creating a really massive ripple.

There is a palpable exhilaration that can be felt during a U & Improved graduation, and as the newest graduates mingled with their friends and loved ones, giving out congratulatory hugs and taking commemorative photos that Sunday afternoon, my head was spinning. *What had just happened?* Individuals and companies alike wanted to pay it forward, to share the important lessons they had learned during their journey through our U the Leader class with the next generation. There was something big here . . . and I needed to sort through what I had just witnessed.

———

As the months went on, inching us closer and closer to the launch of our very first U the Teen Leader class, and as we continued to work away at making U the Teen Leader everything it could be, making small tweaks and refinements as we went along, ordering and preparing for all of the supplies and logistics to bring each of the activities and processes to life, we were quite simply exhilarated! I had pictured this weekend in my mind's eye for months and months now, and the date on which it would all happen was just about here. As that first weekend of August approached, the nervous energy coupled with so much excitement (a feeling my girls aptly named *nervcited* when they were itty-bitty kiddos both anxious and excited about going on their first little roller-coaster ride) was hitting us all. We knew in our hearts that it was ready, that WE were ready . . . but were these teens ready for what was coming their way?

The lobby of the conference room portion of the hotel was abuzz. Staff was arranged at two check-in tables, one for the adults who were getting ready to embark upon their journey into U the Leader and one for the teens and their parents, who were standing in line ready to check their precious cargo, their babies, in to a brand-new experience that they knew would be powerful and amazing, despite having no idea what to expect. Dozens of alumni stood at the ready, willing to assist with any need that could possibly come up. They were, and are, the lifeblood of what we do, and having them there just willing to contribute in any way made us all feel like we were enveloped in a warm, fuzzy blanket on a cold winter's day.

Both of the ballrooms were set and ready, identical to each another, the chairs all arranged in a *U* shape, the trainer's table set and ready to go in the front of the room, the logistics tables in the back arranged with all of the necessary tools, from notebooks and paperclips, to iPads and speakers, to pens and peppermints. We. Were. Ready.

The adults were busily getting checked in, and the parents and teens were doing the same. I had a flashback to what my face must have looked like on that very first day I dropped Alex off at kindergarten. Both my facial expression and my girls' expressions were full of anticipation, excitement, nerves, and hopefulness. The parents today were encouraging their teens and wishing them well, but the teens' faces didn't look like Alex's or Iliana's or any of those little kindergartners' faces I remembered . . .

These faces were not too happy. Some were even flat out pissed. Most of them had zero desire to spend a weekend in some dumb leadership class. And getting up early didn't sound like fun, nor did sitting in a class all weekend long when they could be hanging out with friends or playing video games. And what . . . what was this? They were going to have to leave all of their electronics with their parents??? No phones, tablets, nothing??? Oh, the level of pissed just escalated. While the parents knew about the "no electronics" rule we had put in place for the teens, many or most decided not to share that bit of information with their kids. And anger began to set in on those kids' faces.

"What do you mean I can't have my phone? I HAVE to have my phone. You don't understand!" I heard one boy say.

"I'm gonna lose all my 'streaks'! Mom! You can't take my phone . . . you don't get it!" said another girl.

Ah, and so it begins, I thought. The disconnection from the lifeline that isn't a lifeline but simply a tool. A tool that has become the backbone of their existence. Little did these teens know that, over the next two days, they were going to find the backbones they already had within them.

One boy sat crouched in the corner of the ballroom after he mumbled a quick goodbye to his mom with a noncommittal half hug. He pulled his black hoodie up over his head and stared down at his shoelaces, so mad at what she had just done to him. I could see his fear, and it wasn't just about what lay ahead for him that weekend. It was fear of his potential. He hadn't met the man he could someday become . . . but he was about to.

Another girl looked hesitantly around the room and then timidly seated herself in a chair, awkwardly answering the questions of another girl who sat nearby and was just as uncomfortable. She appeared to be seeking an ally among these teen strangers, some kind of a familiar face she could feel a little comfort from. She didn't see her greatness in that moment, how she could go out of her way to include other people and bring them in, but I saw it.

They all began to get settled in, most not making any eye contact, a few seemingly excited, but the majority wishing they were anywhere but here.

As the last of the parents departed, we were ready to begin. All of the adults were gathered around tables in one half of the check-in ballroom, while the teens were all on the other side of the room, seated around tables of their own. And then the trainers walked in . . .

With booming, confident voices in full projection they marched out, making their introductions and letting the groups know the class start time and where their respective ballrooms were located.

"You've got to be joking . . . ?" one teen whispered to another.

"Why am I HERE?" another said under his breath.

Ohhhh, I thought to myself, *that question, and so much more, will be uncovered for you this weekend, sweet boy. Just trust the process.*

———

The weekend unfolded one process at a time, and, as expected, the awkward and uncomfortable feelings that both the teens and adults were feeling on Friday night were slowly fading away as trust and friendships were being built.

I would bounce from ballroom to ballroom checking on all of my little chickens, wanting so badly to be in two places at once and to not miss a thing. The adults were challenging each other, pushing each other; strangers on Friday night were now a rock-solid team as they worked together through the final transformation of Sunday morning. Tears of joy, exhilaration, and freedom, from the limiting beliefs they had been carrying around for a lifetime, were being shed. It was, as it always is, pure joy from the heart.

In the teen ballroom, the same emotions were being felt. The tears were streaming down cheeks. The cheering and the support for one another made it feel like watching the winning team at the Super Bowl. But this was no game; these teens were getting it. They were getting that it was so . . . much . . . more.

U the Teen Leader, much like our adult U the Leader course, was specifically curated to take these teenagers on a journey—a journey to meet their potential, their best selves. Throughout the journey of the weekend, the teens were faced with a series of leadership challenges. Whether through an activity involving playing cards or strings, some kind of an impromptu speech, or a trust-building exercise, we guided these teens out of their comfort zone and into personal growth and change. As they broke through their mental blocks, all those ideas and limiting beliefs that had been holding back their confidence, their self-esteem, their ability to be optimistic or enthusiastic about their lives and futures—whatever it was for each of them—they faced that fear that had been stifling them. As they crushed those doubts and fears, they simultaneously broke down their walls. They knew it and could feel it as it was happening. The entire experience is always so real, and raw. Each time we experience this course with the teens, we see them accomplish this: overcoming challenges and embracing who they are. They feel the love; they feel the support. They recognize that they are not alone. They have just entered the world of opportunity . . . the world of possibility. They have just entered . . . life.

As graduation approached that weekend, the energy in the ballroom became electric. The teens and adults now sat intermingled at lunch, talking WITH one another. Yes, teenagers and adults, all of whom were strangers a mere forty-eight hours ago, sat together sharing their stories, their takeaways, and their dreams for their futures.

The clock ticked away and as the lunches were cleared, the students prepared to enter the large ballroom together. One big U of chairs replaced the two, as the teens and the adults all sat together, ready to complete their final process, to declare to the audience, and the world, who they were NOW. What they WILL do, who they WILL be, what they WILL have . . .

Dozens and dozens of past graduates filed in; the excitement on their faces was priceless. Truly, I had never seen a room of happier adults in my life.

Graduation began and the room was on fire with passion. Teens and adults alike jumping out of their chairs, sharing what they WILL do differently, how they WILL show up for those they love, how they WILL make a difference in their families and in the world. And all of their joy and passion was mirrored by the applause and cheers of the two hundred people there to cheer them on every step of the way.

It was now the time in the graduation ceremony when the graduates had the opportunity to share any of their thoughts and feelings with the audience, and, just like popcorn kernels, they began to spring from their seats. The first teen to bounce out of his chair to speak was that same young man who sat nestled in his hoodie, staring down at his shoelaces, just two days prior.

"Mom!" he exclaimed, "I know how hard you work. I get it now! I know Dad walked out on us and how hard it's been on you having to do it all on your own, and I just want you to know, Mom, I'm ready to step up and be the man of the house!" he boomed.

The room exploded in cheers, and tears.

Another boy pounced from his seat like a lion ready to attack his prey, but it wasn't prey he attacked—it was the mindset that had been robbing him of his future.

"This class will do one of two things!" he shouted. "It will either change your life or it will save your life. And this class just saved . . . my . . . life . . ." he continued to speak, through his tears.

There weren't enough tissues in the room to absorb all of the emotion that was being felt in the room that afternoon.

And this was how it continued: teens and adults stepping into and up to the best versions of themselves, ready to create the BEST versions of their lives. It was nothing short of awe-inspiring.

For weeks and months following, our alumni buzzed with talk about what they saw and felt that day. The magic they had witnessed. The stories told about what they had done since graduating. One boy, who was being raised by his grandmother and had no future in mind because he couldn't imagine *living* his life, let us know that he was now an enlisted Marine. Another girl shared that because of her U the Teen Leader experience, she loved what she saw when she looked in the mirror, when all she used to see and feel was disgust. She was going to go to college and pursue her dream of becoming a nurse. She saw a future, a future where she was the star.

We were all seeing and feeling it in real time. The impact was there, and young people were feeling the confidence, decisiveness, and passion that we had seen the adults experience over the years since we set out on this crazy adventure of impacting the world. And as those months went on, I knew that the seed the very first graduate had planted in my heart when he proclaimed his desire to sponsor a teen needed to be watered . . .

So I set out to make it happen. I didn't know anything about starting a nonprofit organization, but what I did know was that I would figure it out. There were individuals and companies with huge hearts that clearly wanted to give this next generation of leaders the skills and tools they needed and deserved in order to flourish in life, and there were certainly teens that needed and deserved a helping hand—to see their worth, their value, and their importance.

And eighteen months later, the paperwork arrived in the mail, stating that the U & Improved Leadership Foundation was an official 501(c)(3) charitable organization. The first pebble had been cast by that gentleman a couple of years prior when he stood up and said he would like to sponsor a teenager. Now, upon reading this document from the state of Arizona, I knew that we were about to create ripples far and wide, and I was over the moon with excitement and pure, unbridled joy. I knew from those early days of being a newly single mama that my new title was *role model for my girls*, and now we were going to empower not just adults but also deserving teenagers to become role models in their own families and communities. This was my *why* coming to fruition before my very eyes on a simple piece of government letterhead.

———

As the months continued to tick away, I formed a board of amazing graduates and we got to work. We talked with people and shared the vision. Incredible individual alumni, and corporate clients with hearts of gold, contributed their time and talents—and tremendous financial support. Additionally, we began partnering with organizations that worked with teens: foster care programs, LGBTQ+ groups, anywhere we could think of to find those incredible young people that didn't see or feel their worth. They hadn't had it easy; they felt "less than." These were the kids we were seeking, and we began to find more and more of them.

The months have now become years, and we have been able to provide roughly a hundred scholarships to teenagers across the country through the amazing support of the community; it's a number I am certain will continue to grow and grow. I never sought out to create a foundation, yet it sought me out through the power of one giving heart so many years ago. And it continues, year after year, class after class. Not only do I see the impact in the lives of these children, most of whom I don't personally know, but I also see the power of what we teach in my own home, with my own daughters.

———

When my girls each turned fourteen, they knew it was their turn. Alex was nervcited about the class when she packed her suitcase for the weekend. Iliana was just plain nervous—the excitement wasn't part of her lead-up to class; she was just scared of what was to come.

Each of my girls took several lessons from their individual class experiences, but I got to see it firsthand, in action . . . in their lives.

When Alex graduated from her U the Teen Leader class, she had a solid group of middle school friends that she had grown close to over the two years prior. They spent quite a bit of time together and she was excited for the next chapter of her life to begin: high school.

One weekend in late September, about seven or eight weeks after the school year had begun, I was training for a corporate client of ours down in Mexico. Alex and Iliana were home with my dad, who was helping to take them to and from school and doing all of the things I would be doing for them had I not been traveling.

That Friday night, Alex was heading out to one of her first high school football games. She was so excited to go to the game, to get dressed up with her friends in their school colors and have a blast together.

But this game was different. Alex was at the football game, having a great time with her friends, when some of them decided they wanted to leave and walk over to the drugstore down the road. Alex was perplexed. Should she go with them, knowing she told her Poppy and me that she was only going to the game and then would just need to be picked up by Poppy when it wrapped up? The other girls knew their parents wouldn't approve of them leaving the game and taking off on their own, and they also knew that all of us parents now had tracking apps on their phones, so they couldn't leave without being caught. Several of the girls called their parents, lying to them and saying they were having a great time at the game to throw their parents off. Others disabled their tracking app and planned to claim it must have had a glitch.

None of it felt right or good to Alex. My girls and I have had MANY conversations over the years about trust: how trust is the foundation of every relationship and how there IS no relationship without it. I had drilled it into their heads, ad nauseam, that they were always to tell me the truth, even when they messed up and made a bad choice, because a lie would get them into far worse trouble with me than any action ever could.

She was conflicted. All of her friends were going. She wasn't sure why they wanted to leave and what was happening over at the drugstore that was so important, but she felt uneasy. She called my cell phone, but I didn't pick up. I was in the middle of Mexico with spotty reception and never even heard the phone ring. We had already spoken prior to the game, so I knew where she was, and I'd let her know that I would call her before I headed to bed and to make sure we connected once she was home.

Alex felt desperate, not knowing what to do. Her friends were beginning to leave and as she followed, she felt more and more uncomfortable. She decided to call my dad.

"Poppy . . ." she said softly into the phone, so the others wouldn't hear. "Can you come pick me up now, please?"

My dad was confused and asked her what was up and why she wanted to leave. She just said, "Poppy, please come get me."

He was on his way.

She let the girls know that she couldn't go. Her grandpa said he needed to come get her now from school so she was going to hang back and wait for him.

The girls started in . . .

"Why aren't you coming, Alex? Come on, it will be fun . . . We know you don't have to go home, Alex. Why don't you want to come with us?" they kept on.

She stood her ground. "No, that's okay . . . I'm good."

They began to laugh at her and make fun of her for staying back and for not wanting to tell a little lie and just leave and go have fun with them.

Her heart ached. She didn't know if she was making the right decision, but she was beginning to feel like maybe these girls weren't the same sweet girls they were last year. She got picked up by Poppy and simply told him her friends were all leaving and she just wanted to go home. She called me the moment she got home, in tears about the whole situation.

We talked and talked and I assured her that she did the right thing. She made the right decision and she should be proud of herself.

The following Monday, Alex returned to school, and the girls were . . . ruthless. All of a sudden, Alex had a target on her back. Because she chose not to follow them, they cut her off and out. And while she'd had a feeling on Friday night when she made the decision to leave that that might be the end of these friendships, she had no idea of the nastiness these girls were capable of. They teased her, excluded her; they did everything you would hope your children would never do to someone else.

We never found out what happened at the drugstore that night, if anything. And truth be told, it didn't matter. Alex trusted her gut; she led and didn't follow, and she did what was right for her. She realized that these girls weren't true friends, because true friends would never treat her that way. As the next couple of months went on, there were lots of tears and sadness and much hurt, disappointment, and loneliness as she navigated those first few months of high school having left her friend group to live her life the way SHE wanted to. It was bold, and it was scary, yet as time went on, she began to make new friends and reconnect with others.

One day, as we were driving in the car together, we began talking about all that she had been through and how tough it had all been. She told me how hurt she had been, and how mean these former friends really were to her. She told me how grateful she was to have seen it when she did and to have walked away.

"Mom, you know there is NO way I would have left my entire friend group if I hadn't gone to U the Teen Leader, right?" she said.

I was stunned, totally taken aback. "Really?" I said. "You think it really helped you in making that decision?"

"Mom . . . for sure. Do you honestly think I would have had the confidence to just walk away from ALL of my friends like that? I knew they were going down a bad road and I just didn't want any part of that," she continued.

My heart was swelling inside my body.

A real-life example, in my own daughter, of the impact of the work we do. Wow . . . just . . . wow.

And it didn't stop there.

Three years later, it was Iliana's turn to venture off to her U the Teen Leader experience, but this daughter of mine had zero excitement, only fear.

"Mom, I don't want to do this. Please don't make me go" she said.

She knew there was no negotiating, and deep down she knew it would be a great thing, but in the lead-up to the class, the anxiety was high and she wanted to bolt.

Iliana had made it known to me for years that she couldn't understand how I could possibly enjoy speaking in front of other people. How I had actually chosen THAT, of all things, as my career?

Each school year, when she would have to stand in front of the class and do her "About Me" presentation, I would hear, "Mom, it's AWFUL! I HATE speaking in front of people! It's terrifying!"

"It's okay, honey. I know you don't enjoy it, and just like anything, the more you do it, the easier it becomes" I would reiterate. It fell on deaf ears. Speaking in front of people terrified her, and I knew it was exactly that that was creating all of this nervousness for her. She knew that U the Teen Leader was going to push her to speak, repeatedly, in front of people, and she wanted no part of it.

"You got this, baby!" I told her as she entered the ballroom, getting ready to sit with the other anxious teens who also didn't want to be there. It was a copy-and-paste scenario every time; the majority of teens didn't want to be there on Friday night of class, but still had to sit there, fretfully awaiting their fate.

Iliana was no different. "Yeah, thanks Mom . . ." she said with a smile, half laughing and half ready to kill me, her hands nervously fidgeting with the string of her hoodie.

And as expected, my youngest daughter emerged that Sunday afternoon at graduation projecting her voice, her dreams and goals to the packed room of supporters, filled with uproarious applause.

Iliana began her second week of high school the Monday following her graduation from the teen leadership class. Later that same week, she told me about a presentation she was going to have to give in one of her classes the following week.

I asked her how she felt about it . . .

She said, "Good."

And that was that. I forgot about the presentation because she didn't mention it to me again. No talk of nerves, no dread. It fell off my radar completely, as it was simply a fleeting comment a week or so prior.

The next week, as I was sitting in a client's office waiting for them to come in for our meeting, my phone showed I'd received a text from Iliana.

"Mom . . ." it read. "You remember that presentation I told you about? Well I just presented it . . . LIKE A BOSS!"

I threw my head back in laughter and pure joy! "That's my girl!" I wrote back. "You are a LEADER!"

"Talk to you more about it after school," she replied.

That afternoon I couldn't get home fast enough.

"Tell me ALL about it!" I exclaimed as she and Alex walked in the door from school.

"Well, the teacher asked if anyone would volunteer to go first so I just said I would. And then I went up there and just . . . did it! It wasn't a big deal at all, Mom; I wasn't even nervous! And guess what? He even gave me extra credit for going first because he said no one ever just volunteers right away like that!" she said with pride.

The pride was mutual. I was overjoyed, not for me, but so proud to see HER proud of HERSELF. *That's what it's all about,* I thought. If she takes absolutely nothing else from her class, if that was the ONLY thing she received, wow . . . what a gift that will impact her for the rest of her life.

Year after year, these teens continue to amaze me. They walk through the doors of the hotel ballroom scared and unsure and walk out with the conviction and confidence of a lion. *This* is the ripple effect. They are casting their own stones into their own ponds to see the ripple effect play out in their lives.

Since creating U the Leader to U the Samurai, I was now experiencing the full picture of what it looked like to claim my confidence, communicate to build trust, envision my dreams, and latch on to an infinity symbol that would anchor me to serve the world and make it better. It had all come full circle, or, I should say, it became that endless loop and flow of life. Perhaps you remember that in U the Samurai, we have this image of an infinity symbol emblazoned on the final virtue stone that our students emerge with upon graduating. This infinity symbol is a reminder to seek opportunities to—somehow, someway—continue to leave their mark on this world, leaving it better than they found it. U & Improved is MY infinity symbol that I wish to continue to share with the world. With the creation of U the Teen Leader, I got to see teens and adults alike waking up to possibility and their potential, finding their confidence and conviction, and choosing to live their lives on their terms—with heart, body, and soul.

Dear U,

I never set out to work with teenagers ... or to create a foundation. Those were byproducts of choosing to live moment by moment, trusting the process, and letting my life unfold while simultaneously trusting my intuition to move forward on things that simply felt like the best next step. This "fourth child" of mine, U the Teen Leader, came to fruition simply because people wanted *more*—more life, more joy, more skills, and more tools. And when I heard them, I knew what I needed to do to make that reality come to life and create a ripple effect in the lives of others.

So I ask U, dear reader, when your last day comes, what mark is it that U will wish U had left on the world? What's your infinity symbol? **This isn't about creating something grand and monumental—this is simply about U attaching your actions to your greater purpose—your *why*.**

Simon Sinek, one of the greatest critical thinkers of our time, did a TED talk and wrote a book, entitled *Start with Why*, about his years of research and investigation into a concept he created called The Golden Circle. This theory encourages U to start from the inside out. "People don't care what you do, they care WHY you did it," he continually reiterates.

And I have found that concept to not only be true in my life, but also true of the entire essence and basis behind the work we do within my company. **It's all about the WHY. Leading with the heart, in business and in life.** It's about caring, listening, actually giving a shit about people, the planet, and things outside of our own myopic little bubble that we all live in.

So to help get U started on your journey of uncovering your own passion and purpose, if U don't yet have clarity around this vitally important thread that U can weave throughout your life, I ask U to spend time journaling about your *why*:

WHY do U do what U do? U wake up each morning to do *something*. U have chosen some kind of a career or path ... Why this one?

Does what U do for a living match your passion, or is it simply a means to an end? If it isn't your passion, why not? Remember, life is so very short. There's no time to waste spending your days living a joyless existence. U want to *live* out the work U get to do each day. If U don't, consider ways to make your work more meaningful or how U might choose a new direction in your work and your life.

When U take your last breath on this earth, how would U like to be remembered? What words do U want people to share about U? What kind of legacy do U want to leave behind? What U do on this earth—in this time that U have—matters.

If you lean into your *WHY*, the impact U create will be felt far and wide, for generations to come, leaving an indelible mark on the lives of those U love and perhaps on those who have never even met U. Perhaps it begins with your family or through the work U do. Perhaps it's with a hobby or side hustle that fills your heart and soul, doing something U truly love.

Whatever it is for U, identify it. What is that *WHY*, that driving force—that thing that can get U up early and keep U up late. Identify it and grow it. We only have one shot at this thing called life, as far as we know, so as Nelson Mandela said, "Why settle for a life that is less than the one you are capable of living?"

Be the catalyst.
Cast the stone.
Watch the ripple.

With love and gratitude,

CHAPTER TEN

Slow the F*** Down

Nothing ever goes away until it teaches us what we need to know.
—Pema Chodron—

I was never an actual athlete. Sure, I did some dance and gymnastics as a young child. I picked up snow skiing when I was in high school and played a mean game of badminton back on the JV team, but an athlete? Someone who eats, sleeps, and breathes their passion for sport? Yeah, not so much.

But, for some reason, as I entered the world of personal and professional development in my early twenties, I also found my competitive side. For me, it wasn't about competing with others, as that was reserved solely for board games with my brother and *Categories* games around Suzanne's table. No, this was a different type of competitiveness I was noticing within me—a competition with *myself*. It was about becoming better than yesterday—the evolution into my best self, mentally, emotionally, and physically.

Once the girls and I moved into my childhood home, it was time to get reacquainted with the neighborhood, and one of my first goals was to find my new gym. Up until this point, I had belonged to various gyms where I would go and work out on my own, setting up my own routines or perhaps meeting a friend for a workout. But I am an extrovert at heart; I love the energy of people, and I began to notice that I longed for more of a group fitness experience. I wanted both the camaraderie of being in it together as well as the push and encouragement that only a coach can give.

Eliza, who is always researching, reading, and investigating the latest on, well, *everything*, had told me about how much she loved Orangetheory. At that time, Orangetheory was a newer workout concept in which an instructor leads a class of up to twenty-four people through an intense and super-rigorous workout. Half of the class was spent doing cardio: walking, jogging, running, sprinting, climbing hills or inclines, or a combination of these elements. There was also time spent on the rowing machine, getting your heart rate elevated. The other thirty minutes of class focused on building strength: lifting free weights and doing body weight exercises. It was an incredible mix of movements that keeps your body guessing and avoiding the dreaded "muscle memory" issue, where results diminish because your body adapts to doing the same routine or workout over and over again.

Although Eliza had mentioned it to me before, I had avoided testing out Orangetheory because there wasn't a location convenient to the home we had been renting, but now, with this move to my "new" old house, I noticed that a brand-new Orangetheory location was just opening up within walking distance. I figured it was a sign, so off I went to take my first class.

I walked in a newbie and walked out a "Founding Member." Yup, it was love at first workout. This type of exercise class was so intense, so challenging, so high energy, so . . . fun! I was hooked, and that began my love of Orangetheory Fitness.

The love affair lasted for years and is still going strong today. But when I think back to why this workout facility just clicked so well for me, I realized it was because it was an escape.

As both a single mother and a business owner, I am making decisions and calling the shots all day long.

"Mommy, what are we having for dinner tonight?"

"Jodi, what training topic do you feel is the best fit for our upcoming annual retreat?"

"Mom, can you help me figure out the key points to make for my argumentative essay for English class?"

All. Day. And if you are a single parent, and an entrepreneur, you probably understand what I am talking about. It can become . . . exhausting. And while I would choose this way of life one hundred times out of one hundred, sometimes I simply don't want to make any more decisions or think my way through anything, big or small. I want an escape from decision-making, to let go of the control and just simply *be* for a minute.

Enter Orangetheory.

From the very first class. I saw that I didn't need to think about what to do; they TOLD me what to do every step of the way, literally and figuratively. I was only in charge of the moment I was in. I didn't need to think about or concern myself with what was next; I just had to show up and do what I was told by my coach. Awesome: an hour of turning the logical side of my brain off and turning my *mindset* up to full blast. I got to use my powerful mind for an amazing purpose: to get me through each physical challenge I was directed to meet at that moment. It was fabulous.

This was my morning escape for years. I would run, and then I would run faster. I noticed that was where my competitive side truly came out—on that treadmill. If I could run at *that* speed for *that* long, then surely I could run just a tiny bit faster for a tiny bit longer. My endurance was building, as was my strength, my power, and my speed. I felt invincible when I was in there, pushing myself, with encouragement from the coaches, for just a little more.

"C'mon . . . it's just thirty seconds! You can do anything for thirty seconds!" she would shout.

"Do you have anything left to give? Just a little bit more? Fifteen seconds, this is it! You got this!" the coach would continue.

And I would always dig deeper. And I would always find more. I knew from all that I had been through and all that I had learned through my years and years of personal development that mindset truly IS everything. I always share with our students and my own children, "What you focus on grows." I was focused on becoming stronger and leaner and healthier than ever. That way of thinking is what I preach AND practice. I HAD this Orangetheory thing. I HAD this workout thing. I was getting stronger and more powerful, and I loved that feeling so . . . damn . . . much.

———

In late October of 2018, we were set to head up to Prescott for our next U the Samurai class. Because U the Samurai only took place once a year, it was a very special event—as it still is today!—and there was a big buzz among the U & Improved team and the alumni base as the weeks and days leading up to class approached.

This time was no different. Deno, our fearless U the Samurai lead trainer, was all set and ready to go, as were Dean and I and all of our incredible internal support team. I was going hard during the few weeks leading up to class with several corporate trainings and out of state travel, which meant late nights and early mornings of review and prep work, as well as long days of boarding flights and catching planes. But, as usual, it was nothing that my morning coffee and a good workout couldn't fix.

I had been noticing recently that my legs felt so tight. My hamstrings were especially sore, so I was doing my best to stretch and stretch, but patience is not a virtue that I will be remembered for, so a quick half-ass stretch after a workout and before bed was about all I would make time for. As much as my leg muscles ached, I reminded myself of the old adage from the '80s, "No pain, no gain," figuring I was getting stronger and, in order to keep doing so, I needed to push through this tight muscle feeling so I could keep maximizing my results. So I headed to the gym, got in a workout, then showered and grabbed some lunch with Dean and Deno before heading to the hotel to get U the Samurai, 2018 edition, started.

The first night of class went great. Everyone was all in from the moment they bounded into the lobby. These leaders had already graduated from the first three U & Improved classes, so by this point they were ready and excited to climb to the pinnacle of success mountain.

After our exceptional evening, we all headed up to Prescott, Arizona, the following morning for the remaining day and a half of class. We were pumped—the magic, yet again, was unfolding before our eyes.

The elevation in Prescott is a lot different than in Scottsdale. In the past, every time we drove from Scottsdale to Prescott, I could feel the effects of elevation on my lungs, a noticeable shortness of breath. And this visit was no different. When we arrived, I started recognizing that I had to work a little harder to catch my breath. Again, nothing too unusual and nothing to spend any time focusing on—we had a powerful class to continue to deliver!

We were running fast and hard, the trainers, volunteer assistants, and support staff. There are so many logistics and moving parts to our classes—so many details to consider—that it takes our full energy and attention to make sure everything goes flawlessly. I was running on coffee and a protein bar . . . and more coffee, and even a bit more coffee.

As much as I enjoy my morning cup of coffee or two, I was really guzzling it that weekend because we had late nights and early mornings to contend with, and I wasn't about to miss a second of it.

As the final day of class rolled around, I was feeling depleted of sleep but full of energy. The buzz of the caffeine was nothing compared to the electricity I felt inside from watching this tribe step into their next level of leadership, as samurai warriors of their lives.

Graduation was about to begin. Unlike our other classes, our U the Samurai graduation took place outside, in a beautiful natural-stone seating area surrounded by the lush green pines and gorgeous gigantic rocks. As a surprise to all of the graduates-to-be, past U the Samurai graduates were invited to come make the drive up to Prescott to be there to sit among the giant stones, supporting the newest samurai and celebrating them and their completion of this amazing four-part journey.

As the training team and I headed up from the grassy course where we wrapped up class and made our way up the hill to the graduation area, all the coffee was catching up to me, and I quite simply HAD to pee.

But the graduates were headed up right behind me and the graduation ceremony was going to begin in about five minutes. The restrooms weren't all that close to where the outdoor graduation site was located so I shouted out a quick hello and waved to all of the alumni perched among the giant stones, snapped a quick photo of them all to capture the moment, and then I shouted a quick, "I'll be right back!" as I darted off to the restrooms.

I didn't come right back.

Sprinting as fast as I could off to the restrooms, I didn't make it more than fifty yards before I felt a crippling pain in my left hamstring, immediately followed by a matching pain in my right. It was the pain of ten thousand charley horses happening simultaneously in both legs—the pain of a million knives being stabbed into the back of my legs, the pain of being wrapped in barbed wire by foreign assassins, or needled with electric waves of shock, and then being dropped in the deep, blue sea. Okay, not that last one, but you get the picture. It fucking *hurt*. Badly. I screamed at the top of my lungs as I instantly collapsed onto the concrete pathway.

I screamed and moaned in complete shock over the most excruciating pain I had ever experienced. I couldn't move and I was so confused at what was happening to me. Suddenly, I saw Tiffany and a handful of other alumni there above me.

"Are you okay???" they clamored.

"Oh my gosh, what happened? Did you twist your ankle??"

I could barely speak. I just cried and moaned and couldn't even explain what I felt, beyond just asking that no one touch my legs and saying that something had happened to my hamstrings.

"Oh, maybe she tore her hamstring . . . oh gosh, that is so painful . . ." I heard someone say.

The next thing I knew, Dean had come over and ushered everyone back to the graduation site, comforting me by saying, "Deno and I have graduation handled. Tiffany and Skip are here with you . . ."

He knew I must have been nervous about the timing of this, not wanting to upset the graduation celebration.

Tiffany and her husband, Skip, slowly and gently got me to my feet. The paramedics were already on their way. As I stood there clinging to Tiffany and Skip and writhing in such excruciating pain, I realized I was scared. Really scared. I knew this was more than a tear or minor injury. Suddenly, I was hit with a wave of nausea. Everything felt really hot, and really cold, and then . . . the world went dark.

Luckily, Tiffany and Skip were on each side of me, holding me up when I fainted, so they were able to hold me and help me avoid collapsing yet again. I regained consciousness moments later, right when a fire truck appeared. The firemen came right over and began asking Tiffany, Skip, and me questions. I could barely speak words that made sense; I just kept saying, "It hurts so badly . . . this is crazy pain . . ."

I couldn't sit. I couldn't walk. I could barely shuffle, so quick-thinking Tiffany and Skip had already pulled their SUV over and the firemen gently laid my torso down in the back seat while they carefully held my legs out straight to assess what could possibly be going on.

They asked if I had eaten or had any water. I mumbled that no, I hadn't had much water at all, just a lot of coffee, and they could tell I was very dehydrated. They began an IV right there in the back of the SUV and as the firemen were working to figure out what could have happened, I continued to explain that the pain was so excruciating I didn't want anyone to touch me.

They suggested that I take the ambulance to the hospital there in

Prescott. I refused. I couldn't be in some strange small-town hospital two hours from my girls. I had to get home. They would be so scared. I was so scared. What the hell had just happened? Why couldn't I walk, and what kind of damage had I just done?

And . . . I still REALLY needed to pee—now more than ever, after having a full IV.

Tiffany. God bless this woman. The only person who could literally hold me up and shuffle alongside me to a bathroom, and then literally hold me over a toilet so I could go. I couldn't bend, so this was the most unusual and awkward moment ever, but it did give a brief moment of comic relief, as we both were in complete shock from whatever the heck had just happened.

Slowly, painfully, they somehow got me into the back of Dean's large SUV and as I laid there, Tiffany helped support and hold my ankles so that my legs could remain straight. She sat crouched on the floor of the SUV for two hours, with a couple of restroom stops (the blessing and curse of the IV), on the way back. I was reflecting back to my labor and delivery classes, just breathing and focusing on anything else I could beyond the pain. At each sketchy rest stop Tiffany held me and helped me, and as I shuffled out, unable to even step up onto or down off the street curbs, I wondered and worried if I had done permanent damage. I was petrified.

They got me home in record time and I did my best to explain to the girls that I had really hurt my legs and was already figuring out what doctors to talk to in the morning. I was taking a few Tylenol to relieve the pain, but nothing was helping. This was unlike anything I had experienced, but I was so happy to be back and to see my girls and my dad. At least now I felt like I could exhale, knowing I was finally home and those that I loved the most were right there by my side.

The pain continued to get worse. The next couple of days were filled with doctor's appointments and X-rays, specialists and MRIs. I couldn't walk and I couldn't sit, but my dad, Tiffany, and another amazing, dear friend, Anna, were shuffling me around town as I lay flat in the backseat of the car.

It was determined by specialists that I had a double hamstring avulsion. Basically, my hamstrings had been hanging on by a thread and as my tired and dehydrated body bolted off to run to the bathroom, they simply snapped like a rubber band. The very, VERY odd part of it all, according to the surgeon, who works with all of Arizona's professional athletes in town and specializes in leg injuries like this, was that throughout his career he had only seen two other people with a simultaneous double hamstring injury like this. And both of them were in their twenties, playing professional football. Go figure.

"This is unbelievable! A forty-six-year-old mom is not my typical patient for an injury of this magnitude. What the heck were you doing?" the surgeon asked.

"I really needed to pee . . ." I said with a sheepish grin. "I was just running off to the bathroom . . ."

After days of discussion, phone calls, and meetings with doctors and insurance providers, I had a big decision to make. And I had to make the decision within only a few days.

Seeing as my hamstrings weren't torn, but rather detached from the bone, I could do one of three things: (1) have them both surgically reattached so that I would have the best chance of returning to full strength and power moving forward, yet risking reattaching muscles that were already tight to begin with; (2) have one reattached and leave the other so that I would have at least partial use of one damaged leg while the other healed; or (3) have no surgery at all, let the muscles scar down and not reattach them, and do a hell of a lot of physical therapy to regain as much strength and mobility as possible. But the window to make this decision was closing because the muscles were already beginning to scar down and as that happens and they get close to the sciatic nerve, surgery becomes less viable as an option.

I spent the next few days lying flat on my back in bed, making phone calls. I talked to more doctors, chiropractors, family friends in the field—anyone and everyone I could ask in order to gather as much information as possible. This was a big decision, one that would forever impact my future. And there were no guarantees with any option. Reattach them and perhaps have constant tightness but the possibility of more power and speed; fix one and not the other and have better use of one leg but risk the unevenness of strength between the two; do nothing surgically, dedicate the next year to physical therapy, and take a long, slow, painful road to recovery, risking the chance of ever running again.

As in the early days of my divorce, I found myself at a critical fork in the road, a road shrouded in quiet moments of reflection. And let me tell you, I was reflecting a lot. As I lay there in bed, unable to do anything on my own (I couldn't dress myself, shower, use the bathroom . . . I was 100 percent reliant on help from others), I thought and thought about this big choice ahead of me. And I made myself one promise.

Jodi, whatever you end up deciding will be the right choice because you will MAKE it the right choice.

This was something that my amazing Dean, trainer and mentor to so many, including me, would often say in relation to life and business decisions: There is no "wrong" choice in life. Make whatever decision seems best, and let it go. You will always MAKE it right.

These were wise words that seemed very fitting at this time. So I promised myself that once I gathered and thought through all of the options and all of the potential outcomes, once I decided, *that was it.* The word *decision* has the root meaning "to cut off all other options," and just like that root definition, *this* is what I would do—cut off all other options. I resolved that I wouldn't second-guess, regret, doubt, worry, or wonder. I would stand tall (that was the one thing I COULD do!) and firm in my choice and move ahead one painful, baby step at a time.

As I reflected on options over those few days, I recognized that having surgery on both legs would put me in a care facility for a couple of months while I regained strength and learned to walk again. *Who would care for my girls? How could I possibly be absent from life for two months like that?* Not an option.

And to have surgery on one leg and not the other? Well, that seemed silly to me: one strong leg, one weaker leg, the potential of doing more damage to the unrepaired leg . . . nah, that just didn't make sense to me.

That left me with option three. No surgery and a ton of physical therapy. But wow, I might never be able to run again. And I loved to run. I would definitely never regain the same strength and power I once had. I asked the doctor more about this option.

"Will I be able to climb stairs and still travel the world? One day when I am older, will I be able to get down on the ground with my grandchildren and play *Candyland* with them?" I asked with tears in my eyes, searching for some reassurance.

"Yes, yes you will," he said calmly, with a smile in his voice. "Your sprinting days would be over, but those things? You will definitely be able to do all of those things."

A short window of time to think. I knew the right decision for me: no surgery. If I could walk and climb stairs and lead a mostly normal life, that was my choice. I didn't have to sprint and run fast. And who knew? Maybe with enough physical therapy I would be able to jog a little bit again in my future. Done. Decision made. As we drove off to physical therapy three times a week, every week, for the next few months, with my amazing friends Anna or Tiffany or my dad shuffling me to and from, I knew that I not only made the right decision, but would also MAKE it the right decision, like Dean always said.

The first time the physical therapist touched my legs I could have cried. Or screamed. Or both. My legs had doubled in size and were so black and blue it looked like they had literally died off . . . it was crazy.

But as with anything, it was itty-bitty, tiny, baby steps of progress.

I would notice small gains.

I could step up onto the curb with a little less help.

I could lie flat in the car but with just the tiniest tilt of an incline up.

I could eat my dinner standing at the kitchen counter, with the family seated at the table in front of me, without having to hold on to the countertop quite as tightly as a few days before.

The progress was slow and steady. And the outpouring of love? Otherworldly. Homemade meals, gift cards, and visits were a daily occurrence. I could hardly keep up with the amount of check-in calls and offers to help in any way. I was floored. My immediate family checking in on and caring for me was one thing. But this? This was unreal. I had U & Improved graduates leaving me homemade meals on the doorstep. Tiffany and Skip offered to move in for a couple of months just to help me while I healed (and while I didn't take them up on that unbelievably kind offer, the fact that they would even consider such a thing left me awestruck). Anna would drive an hour across town multiple times each week to take me another thirty minutes away to physical therapy. One of my most amazing clients, a large national furniture retailer, asked if they could deliver a reclining chair or sofa to help me be more comfortable while I healed. Dean had an adjustable mattress sent to the house and installed for me. A couple from Orangetheory, whom I didn't even know that well, made a massive, delicious meal for my girls and me, and personally delivered it to the house. An alumnus came and actually cooked dinner for us in my kitchen! Anna ordered an outdoor chaise-lounge-type chair for me so that I could enjoy Christmas around the tree with my family. When I say I was showered with love and affection, and the most true and pure heartfelt gestures of caring, it was something I never could have imagined. I was in tears daily; I couldn't believe the amount of love I was being shown, nonstop—how people gathered around to help in such a crucial time in my life.

As I worked from my bed for the next two months and regained bits of mobility as the weeks moved on, I was flooded with appreciation. So much gratitude for the gift and insight I was being given throughout this process. My team at U & Improved just made things happen; we didn't miss a beat. Everything flowed effortlessly without my being there, and my speaking and training events simply got postponed. Everyone understood, everyone was so kind—they made it easy. It was a true blessing, because while all those external responsibilities were shifted for a little while, it gave me the time and rest to turn inward. Life had thrown me a huge curveball, and just as I had in prior curveball moments, I did a lot of reflecting.

Why did this happen? What was the lesson I was meant to learn from all of this?

There had to be a reason. There was always a reason.

And this is what I deduced.

SLOWWWW the FUCKKKK DOWNNNN . . .

Yes, I am high energy. I go, go, go. And I love it. I love living all in, all passion, all heart, body, and soul. However, through my hamstring injury and recovery, I realized that it's also imperative to rest. To listen to my body. To slow down . . . take a break . . . relax. Breeeeeeathe . . .

On that beautiful October day in Prescott, life decided to teach me a lesson that I had been ignoring. I recognized upon reflection that you can't pour from an empty cup. I love to give and live and be doing all the things I love with and for everyone in my life, but life FORCED me to slow down. To get quiet. To read the flashing neon sign it had been sticking right in my face . . .

SLOW DOWN. The world will continue to spin and life will carry on even when you are resting.

This teachable moment gave me profound insight. Invaluable wisdom. So much pain, yet so much gain. I was slower and unsteady on my legs, but I was richer and wiser for the experience. I had learned the lesson I was meant to learn, and I vowed to myself never to forget it.

———

Over the next year, 2019, U & Improved continued to grow, and so did my girls. New clients were joining the U&I family, and the middle school years were well underway for Iliana, while high school had begun for Alex. As I regained strength in my legs, I was able to walk more normally and more confidently, a bit like a newborn colt in those early weeks of recovery, but now I was finally taking to the stage again and able to go on long walks and do strength training.

And while stronger, I noticed that my legs felt different, almost like there was concrete inside of them. They moved and worked, but felt heavy and slow. Speed and power were indeed diminished. But through the miracle work of regular and repeated physical therapy, and with a mindset determined to maximize this window of opportunity to regain my strength, I was even able to jog again. It wasn't fast or pretty, but it was *running*, and for that alone I felt so much accomplishment and fulfillment. I was appreciative. And although I was slower and I wasn't able to focus on my speed and compete with myself from workout to workout like I did in years prior, I was more deliberate. I was able to focus on my body, my healing, and my mind. And while all three continued to grow stronger, so did my gratitude for good health and for all that these vessels we are given, these amazing bodies of ours, are able to provide and overcome.

I recognized and reflected upon the lesson that "nothing is promised" a lot during 2019. The girls and I did a lot more traveling. I have always done my best to give them memories, moments, and experiences, without such a focus on "the stuff," and that was definitely at the forefront of my mind after my injury and through my healing process. Once my legs became strong enough to travel again, we did much more of it, going to Hawaii, California, and New York together. I wasn't going to look back one day when my life was done and say, "I wish we would have . . ." I was determined to look back and say, "I'm glad we did."

In the summer of 2019, we also celebrated a milestone birthday. My Omi was turning one hundred years young. And seeing as that's an age most of us don't achieve, it was certainly a big reason for celebration! That summer, for her birthday on June 5th, ALL of our family came to Scottsdale for a weeklong celebration and a birthday party at my house. Our family may not be big, but it is FILLED with love.

All of our family from Australia came to visit, as did Omi's nephew and his daughter, from Chicago and New York, respectively. My brother and brother-in-law were here from Paris. So family from literally ALL over the world made it to Arizona to celebrate the wonderful lady whom we all adored. And as Omi sat at the head of the table and we toasted to her and celebrated her amazing and full life, we all felt so lucky to be together, as this was certainly a rarity. We talked about how special this time was, how treasured these memories we were making really were, how fortunate we all felt.

Little did any of us know what was to come.

No one did. No one on the planet knew that just a few months after we all were together, this family from all parts of the globe would be ripped apart, unable to see each other for years.

———

In the middle of March 2020, as we were driving back from spring break in California, the news was beginning to unfold. We had heard about some kind of crazy virus that had begun spreading from China into Europe and other parts of the world, but, like everyone else, we had no idea what lay ahead.

On that five hour drive home, everything was changing at warp speed. As we made our way home, bits of information were being parceled out like the trail of breadcrumbs in the story of Hansel and Gretel. We heard that schools would be closed for a week. Then two weeks. We heard that travel would cease for a short time. Planes were being grounded. It was all so odd and almost apocalyptic. Yet, at that moment, an extra week off school certainly sounded good to the kids, as it seemed like an extra week of vacation.

Yet, as we now know, it was no vacation. That week turned into two weeks, then two months, then two years of what was the strangest period of our collective lives on earth. A global pandemic of the COVID-19 virus.

For me, and for us in our corner of the world, things certainly slowed down. And in many ways, the world came to a complete halt. We quarantined. We sheltered in place in our homes. We wore masks the very few times we dared to go out for bare necessities. We stayed six feet apart from each other at all times. Restaurants, gyms, businesses, offices, and most stores were closed, and only "essential businesses" and "essential workers" were able to continue on as "normal." The rest of us? We were clamoring to figure out how to remain connected, somehow, virtually. Obviously, the girls couldn't go to school, as every school was closed while educators and administrators were working diligently and feverishly to figure out how to continue to teach our children in some kind of new, remote manner.

As a public speaker and trainer, every training and speaking engagement I had booked was canceled . . . indefinitely. There were no group gatherings, no in-person meetings, no concerts, no sporting events . . . no gatherings of any kind. Nothing. All I could do was call and check in on my clients, letting them know I was thinking of them, and that I was here if they needed anything. But at that time, it was such chaos and craziness, we were all just searching for answers—even just AN answer—to get us from one day to the next. No one was looking to develop and grow their teams; they were looking at what to do TODAY just to get through it and make it to tomorrow. How to keep their businesses up and running. How to keep their employees paid and safe. How to keep food on the table. How to simply stay afloat as the proverbial flood waters continued to rise.

The girls and I made the most of the quiet time at home. We played a ton of board games, we made crafts and did art projects, and I began to cook new meals and recipes nightly (and if you know me, much like patience, I will NOT be remembered for my cooking). But what I actually came to realize was that cooking was quite enjoyable when there were no time demands and to-do lists, and when pouring myself into a meal was my greatest goal for the day. And when I was rewarded with smiles on my girls' and dad's faces? That was priceless.

As the weeks went on, gyms still closed, I began to go on long walks each morning. It was so wonderful to be outside and feel the wind and sun on my skin after spending so much time indoors before the pandemic. The mornings were quiet. As the girls slept, I found the ritual in my morning walks and they became progressively longer and longer. I felt a sense of solitude and the ability to clear my mind for a bit, a time to accept what was while dreaming of what would be on the other side of all of this.

As my business had hit a dead halt, I realized that all I could control about this situation was my mind. So I focused on exactly that. I popped in my AirPods each morning and flooded my ears with audiobook after audiobook. I was determined to fill my mind with powerful thoughts and ideas while the world around me was so shaky and oh-so volatile.

In those early days of the pandemic, I remember thinking, optimistically, *Well, maybe this is all happening for a reason . . . maybe this all* NEEDED *to happen . . . perhaps this is the great reset button that will bring more humanity back to the world. Maybe this will be just the thing we need to get us all back on track and focused on loving and caring for one another.*

But as the store shelves were stripped of basic necessities like baby formula and medicine and people fought over the last package of toilet paper and can of soup, and as people grew frustrated with Zoom meetings and having to say, "You're on mute, Debbie" a thousand times per day, fear, frustration, anger, and division only grew worse. And stronger. So much so that the world felt uglier than ever.

It became apparent that this wasn't going to end anytime soon. My in-person coaching and training business was all but gone. My life came to a crashing halt, much like the halt I experienced when I crashed onto the concrete below me. I had to keep thinking and growing and figuring out what I could do now, just as I had back then. This time, I had to think further out: it was time to focus on what the world needed, what I could do to support others. I knew my gift was empowering others to think bigger and differently, and I knew it was my time to reinvent the way, the METHOD, in which I did it, even if it was only temporary.

As I walked every morning, I also would talk to my dear friend Anna who, much like me, set her own schedule and was essentially her own boss in the work she did. She, too, was feeling the effects of not being able to do much of anything to grow her business at a time like this, when her clients were doing all they could to keep their doors open.

So on those long morning walks, I would call her. And we would talk, many times, for hours on end. While every basic supply was scarce and the world was shutting down around us, we were grateful to Alexander Graham Bell and for Apple products because we could at least hear and see each other, and all those we loved, even if it wasn't in person any longer. We shared our concerns, our ideas, our hopes, and our listening ears with one another. We brainstormed ideas: What COULD we do to generate an income during an "unprecedented time" like this? What did reinvention look like? How could we adapt our previous way of living, working, and being to move through this time and continue to reach others?

During this same time, the murder of George Floyd occurred, and that was the catalyst for making the whole country go even crazier. How could people stand there and watch this occur? How could a police officer do what he did? Why was this hatred still happening ... for decades and generations? The divisiveness, the hatred, the ugliest parts of humanity were in the limelight constantly, and even the strongest of people found themselves wondering how long this could possibly last and how we could solve this horrible chapter in our history. I didn't have those answers, but I wanted to learn more and figure out how I could do my part in at least some small way.

I was getting restless. My morning walks were a solid ten miles each day. I was absorbing as much positivity as I could (from both Audible and Anna) and I recognized I needed to move into action. This wasn't going to end anytime soon, and while everyone was asking when we'd get back to normal, when we'd return to the way things were, I kept thinking to myself, and reminding others who would listen, that there was no normal to return to. Life had changed forever. WE had changed forever. There was nothing to go back to; it was time to rebuild, recreate, and rebirth ourselves into what was to be.

I decided to make a move. I began writing. I began recording. I began creating an online curriculum for this "new world." While I have always been a live event trainer, I knew that I needed to reach people. I needed to continue to support people. I needed to help people find their way out of the dark and back into the light.

CEOs, business leaders, and even the school principal called me, looking for guidance.

"Everyone wants answers and I don't have any to give!" one would say.

"Jodi, I have to tell you . . . my anxiety is sky-high. I need to talk with you and sort my head out . . ." said another.

"My team is struggling . . . I need to be there for them, and for my family. I'm seriously scared . . . I don't know what to do or say from day to day."

I understood it. I felt it. I was feeling so many of the same emotions, yet I'd been given these tools over the years, and it was time to continue to share them with anyone I could help.

I began doing free weekly online workshops to help leaders strengthen their mindsets through all of this. I created a five-week online course called the Mindset Masterclass in order to share even more mindset tools and build a sense of community when everyone felt so fragmented and disconnected.

And I went back to school. I decided that now was the time to dive deeper into my understanding of equality, diversity, and inclusion, so I did a lot of research and decided to enroll at Cornell University to gain my certification in exactly that. I knew that taking all of these online classes wouldn't stop the hatred and the racism and the ugliness I was witnessing, but I did know that it would provide me with more knowledge and that knowledge coupled with action, actively sharing what I was learning, could at least begin to move the needle of understanding. Even if just one person could be positively affected, all of the months of classes and studying and papers and tests would be worth it.

And along with that, I knew that I wanted to continue to expand my knowledge and understanding of mindfulness—of regular self-care and the active pursuit of mental peace. So I simultaneously enrolled in an online program through Yale University and began my quest to learn more about "The Science of Well-Being."

The pandemic lingered on. However, safety protocols began to shift and allowed us to be around others in very small groups while distanced and masked. I decided I needed to keep my mind sharp and challenge it a bit. I needed to step outside of my comfort zone and push myself to learn and grow in a positive and fun way. What could I do that would provide that though?

Oh . . . yes. That's it! Improv!

I enrolled in a small improv class and got myself wildly uncomfortable by having to think on my feet—faster than I probably ever had to in all my life—and the feeling of challenging my mind like that, after being so focused on the day-to-day drama of life, felt exhilarating.

All of these courses and experiences were fascinating. When I am learning and growing, while creating and helping others, I am at my happiest. It felt like the early days, when I was first introduced to the work of Les Brown, Jim Rohn, and Tony Robbins—that heart-swelling emotion I would feel when I began to expand my mind and heart and realize that anything truly is possible. So although there was little to no income coming in, I was still doing what I loved. I was evolving. And the way I have always seen it, you either evolve or repeat. And there was no chance I was going backward.

Yeah, the income to my business dropped 79.6 percent in 2020. It was ugly. Really ugly. But me? Go backward? Never. I was going to continue to choose the windshield over the rearview mirror.

And what's that old saying? What doesn't kill you makes you stronger? Yeah . . . that one. Well hell, I had been through a lot of struggles in my first forty-eight years of life; this was certainly not going to break me. I'll never forget one time, early on, when U & Improved first started gaining traction, a man came up to me after a speaking event and asked who my partner was (assuming I couldn't have done this by myself). When I told him that I started U&I on my own, he seemed sort of shocked and said, "Really . . . you did this all on your own? Wow, you must have done really well in your divorce!" I was dumbfounded. *If U only knew how far from the truth that was!* So I replied and said, "No . . . actually, I didn't 'do well' in my divorce at all. Actually, my husband stopped paying child support and I have been raising my two little girls solely on my own. And the only business partners I have had are Visa and American Express!" I started U & Improved in the fall of 2008, when the recession was underway and people were being laid off and businesses were in complete turmoil economically. My thought was always *What goes down must come up.* I knew that, in time, companies would desperately need to invest in their people and leaders would need to show those people they are the most valuable asset of the company. And just like in 2008, I knew that this experience in 2020 would be a new fire to burn bright and get me even more creative, more impassioned, more excited about creating something new. We would see our way through, one day at a time. And I would rebuild stronger and better than ever.

So as I built myself up with more knowledge, skills, and mindset tools, I also helped build resilience and confidence in my girls. We talked about how we can do hard things, how every joy and every sorrow is all momentary. How we would get through this dark and challenging time with the lessons we learned etched in our hearts forever, the difficult lessons a reminder of where we had been and how truly strong and capable we are, and the positive moments a reminder of the joy we can choose to create . . . always.

And we did learn these lessons. We REALLY learned them. Once again, I was relearning the *slow down* message. And this time, just like last time, I was forced to slow down, but now I had the awareness to be deliberate in my thoughts and actions—what I chose to do and not to do. I sought out the joy in our "car picnics," when we would pick up food from the curb of our favorite restaurants to support the restaurateurs as they navigated this tough time, and we enjoyed "eating out" in a whole new way. We found the fun in playing games like *Clue* and *Trouble*, laughing so hard as the stakes got "real."

We appreciated our health even more. We found creative ways to stay active and healthy, ordering a double stroller for our two little dogs, who couldn't keep up with our long afternoon family walks (yes, afternoon walks on top of the morning walks!). We consciously thought of others and how we could help and support them through charitable work we could do from home, whether it was note cards and bags of necessities for those experiencing homelessness or bringing food to neighbors and friends who couldn't get out much. And during this time, we visited our Omi for that last year of her life, touching our hands to hers through the glass window of her care home.

The pandemic, while obviously horrific in so many ways, anchored in my mindset the importance of slowing down and becoming more aware and conscious of our own daily desires. It taught me to appreciate the moments differently, to hold on to them even more strongly than I had previously. I was forever changed, just like the rest of the world was. But as I rebuilt my business, as my daughters and I recreated our school and working lives, and as we found new ways to interact and engage with one another and the world around us, I learned a new version of that lesson I learned when I crumbled onto the concrete walkway just a couple of years prior.

Today, I still work out at Orangetheory, much like I did before. However, I no longer compete with my previous speed or distance; I don't do all that sprinting. Now, it's simply about becoming the best version of myself that I can possibly be in this moment. I listen to my body and honor it, unlike before my injury when all I knew how to do was push, push, push. I am more intentional about the movement I give my body, to strengthen and lengthen my muscles, while also creating a space and place for calm presence. Quite simply, I have recognized the importance of being aware, more conscious and more deliberate in my actions, my thoughts, and my spirit. And it all starts from within.

And through all of my life's journeys, throughout these first fifty spins around the sun, I have recognized that my company, my brand, my life's work—ultimately, my life's purpose—is so perfectly fitting to its name, which came to me in a flash so many years ago.

U & Improved.

U & I.

It's all about U . . . & . . . I.

The U is a constant reminder to care for yourself so that you can, in turn, take care of being present for all of the people and moments that matter most to you. You can't give what you don't have—put on your oxygen mask first, baby.

The & is a concept we teach regularly in our trainings and highlights how in life it's not about choosing this or that, either/or. It's about seeking the *and*. How will I have a successful business AND be an active, engaged, and loving mother? How will I impact more and more lives AND take care of myself in the process? These are questions that I have answered for myself by realizing that, through creating work and life HARMONY (not *balance*, but rather *harmony*, because when something is perfectly balanced it doesn't move, and life is in constant movement) I, like you, really CAN and WILL have it all.

The I has always stood for *improved*. However, throughout my evolution as a woman, a mother, a trainer, a coach, an entrepreneur, and a leader, I have realized that the I is more than simply *improving*.

I have learned that the I is about improving INTENTIONALLY—with clarity and conviction. It means taking a look at what "better" means and looks like to you and setting forth the intention to move in that direction, deliberately and consistently. It's about honoring the compass within you, and the core values that anchor you, as you reach for the very best version of yourself.

Intentional improvement is what I will continuously seek and what I will forever help others find for themselves.

It's what I do. It's who I am.

It's all about U & I.

And this has been, and remains, my journey.

From me to U.

Dear U,

The small joys in life: a baby's giggle, one of your team member's big wins, your loved one giving U a kiss on the forehead, cheering on your favorite artist after a performance of a lifetime. They are all just fleeting moments, yet they are, indeed, the essence of life.

Through navigating my hamstring injury and then COVID-19, I learned those important lessons that far too many overlook and perhaps only recognize when it's all too late.

The importance of deliberate, thoughtful action. Intentional, meaningful interactions.

The blessings hidden in the stillness of silence, the quiet, the gift of contemplation and not knowing the answers.

The willingness to trust.

Perhaps much like U, dear reader, I have always moved fast. I walk fast; I talk fast. I've got a lot to do in a little bit of time. And as the sand spills through the hourglass with what seems like ever-increasing speed, I am continually reminded of these important lessons.

Be intentional.

Say what U need to say.

Do what U love to do.

Bring joy to yourself and those around U.

Sometimes in life we are forced to slow down. We are given the proverbial wake-up call. And in 2020, the whole world was given the wake-up call. There wasn't anyone who didn't get the memo this time. But did we all read it?

Oftentimes, it is that kind of forced slowdown that we need in order to speed up. We need to experience "slow" in order to rev up our awareness, our passion, our love for ourselves and others.

So how does a busy person like U actually take the time to slow down? Let me break it down for U:

1. Ask yourself, **"In what area or areas of my life do I need to, and deserve to, slow down?"**

2. **Create a list of what slowing down will actually do for U.**
More focused time and attention with those U love and care

about? Fewer careless errors as U grow your business, so that U can go further faster? Being healthier so that U can stick around for this thing called life a whole lot longer?

3. Look outside of yourself and **identify what slowing down will bring to those U love and care about most.** More mentorship for your employees? More trust and love for your partner, spouse, children, or friends? More engagement within your community?

4. **Reward yourself and celebrate.** Oftentimes, we overlook this step because we have moved on to the next to-do list item or the next task at hand; however, celebration anchors us in the positive emotion and memory of the moment, and that's indeed something to hold on to!

And ultimately . . .

5. **Who will U become in the process?** As U slow down and become more aware and conscious of what U do and how U think, U will naturally grow to understand who U are becoming along the way. U will begin to see those small gains that lead U toward an even more intentional, authentic, and improved U.

I have come to realize that, for me, it's no longer all about the hustle in my life. I spent many years—decades—hustling. And there is a lot of value in hustling: the work ethic, the sacrifice, the personal growth. And I wouldn't change any of it. From the hustle, I learned who I am and what I am made of when I am faced with the challenges and the speed of a fast-moving life. And yes, I still hustle. But I hustle much differently.

Because I have also learned something very important . . .

Alignment is my NEW hustle.

Taking time to nurture ALL areas of my life. Taking time to sit, to sleep, to breathe. Taking time to remember what set my soul on fire throughout the various decades of my life and seeking to recapture those feelings—the joy, the lightheartedness, the carefree and uninhibited spirit, the magic of childhood innocence.

Years ago, when I was a little girl, my father created a piece of artwork for me that still hangs in my home today. It consists of an outline of seven squares stacked in a column; within each square is one little "flag" in a different bright color of the rainbow. The piece is entitled *Joys of Jodi*, and it has hung on my walls and has traveled with me from my dorm room to my apartments and from one house to the next. So perfectly named, my dad's artwork has brightly "flown" as a reminder to me to find joy in EVERY day—in every moment. The joy is ALWAYS there, if U seek it. It's always there if U recognize it. And it is certainly always there if U acknowledge it.

Maybe U don't have a painting in your life that says *Joys of U* to remind U about the importance of finding your joy. But U have this book, and U have me, and so I ask:

What is the joy in your life today? And what will be the joy in your tomorrow? And where and how will U find the joy in your week, month, and year ahead?

I challenge U to become intentional, to seek out the joy, to recognize it and appreciate it. It all goes so fast.

Savor every moment.

Be intentional.

Be grateful.

And most importantly, be uniquely U.

With love and gratitude,

Conclusion

When I reflect back upon my life, I can't help but think of the high-light reel. Fifty years have all but flown by. While I desperately hope that I am just now hitting the halfway point, I know that one day the sand will run out ... yet this book will live on. One day, hopefully, my great-great-grandchildren will come across a dusty old copy of this book, and should they choose to read it, they will gain a little something for themselves, just as I hope you have, my dear reader. (And I suppose, if nothing else, they'll at least get a glimpse into the stories of some lady that they were related to that lived one heckuva crazy life.)

But back to that highlight reel. It's been immense so far. I mean, how can I ever forget winning second place in the third-grade spelling bee? (I will never NOT know how to properly spell *horizon* ever again!)

Or landing my first big-girl internship in the radio industry?

My weddings, the births of my amazing daughters, starting numerous businesses and failing until I created U & Improved, knowing deeply that THIS held my heart . . . this was "the one."

The flash mob that broke out into song and dance (created just for me—can you BELIEVE it?!) at a U the Leader graduation several years ago. (Seriously, one of THE coolest and most special things I have ever witnessed!)

All of the times seeing my favorite artists own the stage—from Billy Joel to P!NK to Neil Diamond (don't judge . . .)—living their purpose before my eyes.

Seeing tens of thousands of graduates consciously choose to live their lives with passion . . . ahhh . . . nothing greater.

The countless awards U & Improved has won for the important work we do, the most recent, and perhaps the most meaningful to me, being the Torch Award for Ethics that we were honored with in the fall of 2021 from the Better Business Bureau of the Pacific Southwest.

All of these moments are just a quick snapshot, a glimpse of the fun from the highlight reel I call my life. For me, these are the moments both big and small that have made the journey of my life so extraordinary.

And the highlights continue to unfold. Today, my incredible daughter Alexandra is looking at colleges and has solidified in her mind and heart that Arizona State University is her next step, while working away at her very first job at Trader Joe's. She loves the people and working there has certainly reaffirmed her desire to always surround herself with down-to-earth, authentic people. My amazing Iliana is kicking butt in high school, continuing to do her best work and wanting to always give it her all, while pedaling her heart out in spin classes that she loves going to several times each week. These girls braved the pandemic, like everyone else, and I believe they became more confident, connected, and resilient because of it. Yes, it was tough, REALLY tough; however, these two girls of mine never cease to amaze me. They constantly looked for the bright side and the lessons they could take from the experience, and their upbeat, playful spirits made a difficult time in life much more palpable. These girls are bold and honest, direct and confident. They are loving and thoughtful, kind and compassionate, and I love that so much about them. They each know who they are, yet they are open to discovering more about themselves as their lives unfold before them.

As for me, I am sincerely loving the work I GET to do each day—coaching, training, speaking—all while watching *a-ha* moments occur before my very eyes. This is the work I am meant to do; I am living my purpose daily. Now, is each day easy or a bed of roses? Hell no! I work my tail off, and . . . there is nothing I would rather do. Ever. I know without a shadow of a doubt that I am exactly where I am meant to be, doing exactly what I am meant to be doing. (Hopefully, here at the end of this book, you also have that spark of purpose . . . perhaps leaning into where you are meant to be or discovering exactly what you are meant to do.)

And, finally, U & Improved. I am proud, and humbled, to say that we survived the chaos of 2020 and came out the other side even stronger and more relevant than ever. As companies are struggling to remain current, navigating through unprecedented times and wondering, now more than ever, how to attract and retain great talent in a lacking workforce, we are here serving these clients, helping to support them as they grow a culture that is truly grounded in heart-based leadership. As more and more companies realize that Ping-Pong tables and beanbag chairs do *not* a culture make, we are here, continuing to do what we know matters and doing what we do best. We are thriving, we are growing, and we are continuously looking forward to a bold and bright future that helps to shape the lives of individuals and the businesses they represent. Making the world a better place, one leader at a time.

Dear reader, before we say adieu, I must impart one final thought, one more bit of wisdom . . . one lasting wish. It comes from the poem below, which holds so much significance for all of our U & Improved graduates, as it is a big anchor in our U the Leader course:

———

The Dash
By Alton Maiden
University of Notre Dame, 1996

I've seen my share of tombstones, but never took the time to truly read,

The meaning behind what is there for others to see.

Under the person's name it read the date of birth, dash(–), and the date the person passed.

But the more I think about that tombstone, the important thing is **the dash**.

Yes, I see the name of the person but that I might forget,

I also read the date of birth and death but even that might not stick.

But thinking about the individual, I can't help but to remember **the dash**,

Because it represents a person's life and that will always last.

So, when you begin to charter your life, make sure you're on a positive path.

Because people may forget your birth and death, but they will never forget **your dash**.

———

May you—yes, U—live your dash.

May U consciously, deliberately, and INTENTIONALLY design a life that makes U happy, and proud, and full of unbridled joy.

This is the essence of life. This is what it's all about.

Enjoy every moment.

From me to U . . .

Hugs (a.k.a. Acknowledgments)

If I could wrap every one of these incredible human beings in a giant hug, I would. Throughout my life, I have always loved the deep, palpable connection that only a hug can bring and the volume of love it conveys. In our classes at U & Improved, hugs serve as a powerful anchor that connects us to one another and to humanity as a whole. So rather than simply "acknowledging" the following people, please allow this to serve as the biggest, most heartfelt hug to each and every one of U.

To my dad . . . the first man to love me and believe in me. Thank U for always being there for me and the girls. Thank U for being my cheerleader, my greatest supporter, and my friend. U are the only one that has known me since the moment I took my first breath, and U have never wavered from having my back since the beginning. Thank U for your love, your support, and ALL of your help over the years. The girls and I owe so much to U, and I know we wouldn't be where we are today without U. Thank U from the bottom all the way to the very tippy top of my heart.

To my brother . . . Marc, U have always been my big brother, looking out for me, giving me sound advice, being our family's living history book—the only person who can know exactly what I am thinking and feeling or what random song or play on words is about to fly out of my mouth (because it's the same one U are about to utter!)! Thank U for always looking out for me, for wanting what is best for me, and for always teaching me, since I was a little girl, to challenge myself to do my very best work. Our bond and friendship is one of the most important and special relationships in my life, and I couldn't be luckier to be your little sis, Sugar Bowl.

And to my bonus brother, Alain . . . I never could have imagined that I would be gifted with a SECOND brother, whom I love as if we had known each other since birth. U are so loving, so supportive, and so MUCH FUN . . . and I appreciate U beyond measure. And besides that, U make the MOST delicious crepes! Thank U for always teaching the girls and me how to appreciate all of the beautiful tastes and sights the world has to offer and for loving and adoring my brother all of these years. And thank both of U for being the two very best uncles to Alex and Ili. They, and I, are so fortunate and so grateful.

To my Omi and my Opi . . . while U are no longer physically here with me, I thank U for teaching me some of the most important principles in life that I carry with me today. Thank U for teaching me to always want to learn and grow, to develop the love of knowledge and the courage to stand up for what I believe in, and to know the importance of putting myself in others' shoes and thus have a compassionate heart for serving those that are less fortunate. Thank U for teaching me to be a hostess, a lady, and a true friend to others. I miss U both every day. However, U remain with me daily through the valuable lessons U taught me that live on in your great-grandchildren today.

To all my family near and far . . . Lisa and Phil; Fiona and Robbie; the extraordinary eight: Rachel, Benjamin, Steven, Mark, Annabel, Simon, Melanie, and Camilla; my incredible cousin Melanie and my uncle George; and, of course, Ileana and David, whom I will forever hold in my heart. I love U all, and while I wish the distance between us all was shorter, I am comforted to know that we all are lucky to have family across the globe that is always there and connected through our heartstrings.

For my dear Penny, Sari, and Mark . . . thank U for being my "bonus family." From laughing 'til we cried (and snorted) to Swensen's ice cream and shopping cart rides, each of U are my extended family and I thank U for being the lead characters in some of my most favorite memories.

To all of my dearest friends, from grade school to today . . . Anna, for your never-ending support and forever friendship. "My Mia" and Shelle . . . for so many years of birthday celebrations, stories shared, and memories made. Jenny, my badass Fire Falcon . . . thank U for your passion, conviction, and tenacity and for being a rock-solid friend for all these years. Eliza . . . for your sound advice and ability to ask the questions that always make me think deeper. Michelle and Gabe, and Andrea and JJ . . . for being there for me through the darkest of days and for so many beautiful years of friendship since. Lisa, Chaz, and Richard, and Mande, Mason, and Mia . . . for being a beautiful extension of our family. The "Decamoms," Tami, Kathryn, Dana, Deena, Jamie, Rachel, Amy, Tarry, and Anita . . . for being there for the highs, the lows, the laughs, and the tears . . . we have shared them all . . . thank U for being the most solid group of mama friends I could ask for. To my first true best friend, Amanda . . . for being one of the most real and authentic human beings I know; I simply adore U and will always be your biggest fan. To my high school besties Jenny, Terrye, Carol, Michelle, Jaime, Steve . . . for lifelong friendships, the silliest of times shared, and always loving me for me. To my ASU Alpha Phi sisters . . . for years of memories and friendship! And to every other friend near and far that has been there on this journey . . . thank U all for being the brightest lights, the best supporters, who love me unconditionally and are always a phone call away. Each of U has been an integral part of my life, and I only hope that I can be the friend to U that each of U has been to me.

To my professors, mentors, coaches, educators, and teachers . . . thank U all for teaching me how to be a critical thinker. Dr. Frederick Corey . . . thank U for helping me learn, back during my college days at Arizona State University, how to share my stories, my voice, and my heart. U were the most impactful professor I ever had the pleasure of learning from. And to Linda Kearns . . . one of my most amazing high school English teachers, who helped me cultivate my love for words, language, and writing.

To Kelsey and my RTC team . . . thank U for helping me bring these stories, and their lessons, to life so that others may find their own North Star, perhaps just a little bit more easily.

To my second family, my U & Improved team . . . Dean, I don't know that anyone has had more faith in my training and speaking abilities than U. U have been a best friend, a mentor, and one of the most important and special people in my life. Without U I simply would not be where I am or who I am today. Thank U for your years of guidance, support, generosity, coaching, and love. I am forever grateful to U, as none of this would be possible without U. Thank U for always believing in me. Deno . . . my wise sage, my Coyote Hawk, who has been there though it all . . . thick and thin. U have always been such an honest, encouraging, and supportive friend and mentor. Thank U for always being a phone call away, time and again, without question. Chris . . . the man who gives the BEST hugs and someone who stepped in and stepped up, at a moment's notice. Thank U for your trust, your willingness to be all in, and the extra special friendship we share. Michael . . . my brother from another mother, the memories we make in front of the room together and when U shape the lives of our future leaders. Thank U for being U and for saying yes to this wild ride we get to take together. Gina . . . whom we all love and miss, yet know without a doubt is with us all in each U the Communicator class we deliver. Your heart and your laugh inspire me and always remind me to focus on joy. Tiffany, my forever soul sister . . . I don't have enough words or pages to thank U for your love, support, friendship, and sisterhood. The memories we share are endless and I can't wait to keep making more. Thank U for decades of friendship that a little ad in the paper brought into my life. I adore U. And Skip . . . thank U for being my lifelong MacGyver and friend, and for always lending a helping hand. Tiffany "TG" and Samantha . . . U help hold down the fort, U make sure I stay on track, U make sure everything gets done, and that all *I*s are dotted and *T*s are crossed. Thank U for having my back and for making all the behind-the-scenes magic happen so that together we can continue to improve lives every day. I would be lost without your help . . . thank U!

And to every U & Improved graduate and client (a.k.a. family) over these first fourteen years . . . I don't get to do the work I do without each of U. Every one of U said yes . . . U trusted me and believed in me . . . and I don't take that lightly. I love U, I appreciate U, and while the list of alumni, clients, and partners is too long to print, know that each of U is etched in my heart forever; through these pages, please feel the good, long, nurturing hug that U each deserve. I am forever indebted to U for your belief in me from the very beginning . . . thank U all.

And finally, a big thanks to U, dear reader, for wanting to be a part of this journey with me. Thank U for being willing to read my words and for traveling through my life's experiences alongside me. Thank U for being open to learning and growing, and thank U for simply being . . . U.

My heart is full. I love and appreciate each of U. With love and gratitude . . . always.

Joys of Jodi

In the spirit of one of the very first pieces of artwork my father ever created for me, *Joys of Jodi*, which consists of seven colorful flags, each one a reminder to bring joy to every day of the week, I wanted to pay this sentiment forward to U. My take on a written version of my father's *Joys of Jodi* provides seven touchstones to refer back to when U want to revitalize and replenish. I know in my life, music, reading, great quotes, and sound advice were some of the elements that got me through the roughest patches and the toughest times.

Below, I have provided U with "a few of my favorite things" (yes, another *Sound of Music* reference), everything from tips to build your confidence to a list of my favorite reads on empowerment and personal development. Each of these seven touchstones brings me joy and helps put a smile on my face. My wish is that they will do the very same for U.

♥ Favorite Reads

Start with Why by Simon Sinek
A powerful book to help identify your personal *why* and/or the *why* behind your business.

The Go-Giver by Bob Burg and John David Mann
A wonderful fable about the power of giving, both in life and in business.

The Gifts of Imperfection by Brené Brown
The most beautiful illustration of the power of vulnerability.

The Four Agreements by Don Miguel Ruiz
Powerful words to serve as a North Star to live by.

The Slight Edge by Jeff Olson
The magnitude of small daily actions, and how they can lead to wild and wonderful results.

"Hug o' War" by Shel Silverstein
One of my favorite poems of all time—simple, powerful, and sweet.

"The Road Not Taken" by Robert Frost
This poem's language is framed so perfectly to illustrate the impact of taking the less traveled path in life.

♥ Quotes I Have Written over the Years

Several of these quotes have come to me in my sleep, and I hurriedly wrote them down, deciphering my own chicken scratch in the morning. Others have been a "brain download" while I was driving, walking, or drifting off to sleep. My Opi instilled this love of quotes in me; they are my comfort, my courage boosters, and my magic. If they provide a bit of inspiration, a moment to pause or reflect, or even a simple smile, then sharing them with U will have been worthwhile.

"When we are grateful for what we have,
While working for what we want,
Fear disappears,
And calm is restored." —Jodi, 2016

"If U can think it,
U can create it.
When U create it,
U will believe it.
When U believe it,
U will become it.
When U become it,
U will soar." —Jodi, 10/26/15

"The get is in the give." —Jodi, 4/3/17

"Use your mind. Trust your gut." —Jodi, 3/14/18

"Your I WILL is more important than your IQ." —Jodi, 2019

"Sometimes U deal the cards. Other times U deal with the cards you're dealt. Either way, you've got to learn to deal." —Jodi, 2009

"Don't LEAVE a legacy; LIVE your legacy." —Jodi, March 2022

♥ Jodi's Playlist

Here's a sampling of some of my favorite songs. Some are favorites for their lyrics, others for their beat. What all of these songs have in common is that every one of them helps me shift my state of being, in an instant. (Hint: find me on Spotify and we can listen to these together!)

PART 1

"So What" —P!NK
"Music of the Night" (*The Phantom of the Opera*) —Andrew Lloyd Webber
"America" —Neil Diamond
"Imagine" —John Lennon
"The Dance" —Garth Brooks
"We Are the World" —USA for Africa, Multiple Artists
"My Wish" —Rascal Flatts

PART 2

"This Is Me" —Keala Settle and The Greatest Showman Ensemble
"The Sound of Silence" —Simon & Garfunkel
"Freedom!" —George Michael
"Survivor" —Destiny's Child
"Man in the Mirror" —Michael Jackson
"Where Is the Love?" —Black Eyed Peas
"Yellow" —Coldplay

♥ Age-Old Wisdom from the Low Family

Here are just a few of the important things my Omi and Opi taught me and would no doubt want U to know!

How you call out into the woods is what gets echoed back.
This is how Omi would say it. *Jodi's translation:* Your actions and your words will always come back to U in some way. Make sure U choose wisely.

Always, ALWAYS put powdered sugar on a cake, and parsley on a meat platter, before serving.
Jodi's translation: Presentation is everything. Put in the extra effort. Make anything U can beautiful.

Never walk across the house empty-handed.
Jodi's translation: Efficiency is key. Kill two birds with one stone any chance U get.

When U wrap a present and put it in a gift bag and U add the tissue paper, thinking U are done ... always add a little more.
Jodi's translation: Life is a celebration ... don't skimp on the fun, and go above and beyond to create a party!

Wash your hands from your fingertips to your elbows.
Jodi's translation: The world is dirty; act accordingly.

Don't walk barefoot in the house; U might step on glass.
Jodi's translation: Be aware of your surroundings, prepare for the unexpected, and just know that sometimes U will get hurt ... and that's okay.

A black or a white horse is not a horse, a horse is a horse.
Jodi's translation: We are a helluva lot more similar than we are different. Embrace diversity—it's what makes the world interesting. Who wants to eat boring old vanilla ice cream every day? Bring on the sprinkles, baby!

♥ Tools to Build Your Confidence

Confidence is the cornerstone of leading a successful business and it is the bedrock on which we build a meaningful life. Without it, we are merely crossing our fingers, hoping for success . . . and hope, my friends, is not a strategy. But with confidence, anything is possible! So here's where to get started:

Watch Amy Cuddy's TEDx talk on YouTube. Learn about the strong connection between our bodies and our minds, the direct effect one has on the other, and the impact the two working in synergy can have on your life!

The power of affirmations and mantras. Our minds believe whatever we tell them. It's not hokey; it's science. Repeat daily: *I deserve good things. Money flows to me. I GOT THIS! Anything is possible!* These are just a few ideas. Create your own powerful mantra or affirmation, and watch the impact that repetition of consciously chosen thoughts has on your results, outcomes, and life!

Envision. Begin with the end in mind. Whatever U are setting out to do, picture the outcome in your mind, as if it has already happened. Dr. Wayne Dyer talks about how we must "feel the feeling of the wish fulfilled." Do it. It works.

Practice, AND be okay with being fluid. Whether U are giving a presentation or have to have a difficult conversation, practice and be clear on the points U are looking to make, but don't go in scripted or memorized. The power of connection comes from authenticity.

Move! Movement is part of our lifeforce. It releases toxins, lessens anxiety, clears your mind, creates more focus, and simply makes U feel like a badass once you're done! Exercise, pace, walk, jump up and down—do whatever U need to do to get your blood flowing and your endorphins going! Work out at least three days per week, MINIMUM, and be sure to move your body in some way daily!

Make the study of personal development part of your daily habits. Be disciplined. Not rigid, but disciplined. U are, and will forever be, your biggest asset. Take care of your mind. Feed it healthy "food." Pay attention to what goes in; as they say, garbage in, garbage out. Choose to feed your mind the best thoughts, ideas, and principles so that U can translate those directly into your life and business.

Make and maintain close friendships in your career and throughout your life. Make this a habit and practice during your entire life, and U will have collected the biggest gift and be forever rich. Relationships are what life is all about, plain and simple.

♥ Little Words of Wisdom from Parenting Two Kiddos on My Own

Being a single mom, I've gathered quite a bit of wisdom on how to navigate the precious moments and pitfalls of parenthood. Here are some of my best tips and tricks:

Make little moments special. Whether it's another Target run or turning takeout into a special "car picnic," turn the mundane into the extraordinary by simply unleashing your creativity. Some of my girls' and my favorite memories have come from the everyday moments that we turned into something special.

Give your kids something to look forward to. This past year, my daughter was struggling with a tough class at school that had her feeling anxious and upset. So every Tuesday and Thursday, I had her draw a number from a bag; each number was correlated to some little grab-bag item—a little something like a pack of gum or piece of candy—to put a smile on her face and celebrate getting through another tough week. Well worth the few extra dollars to help calm her fears and get her feeling strong and focused again.

Ask meaningful questions at the dinner table each night. Since the time my girls were little, I would ask them three questions around the dinner table: (1) What was the best part of your day? (2) What are you most excited for? and (3) What are you most grateful for? The three of us would each share our answers, and it opened up real conversation and instilled gratitude in our day-to-day life. Mission accomplished.

Create a meaningful bedtime routine. Up until their teen years, I would tuck my girls in at night and we would have the same little nighttime routine. I would ask each of them to list five things they love about themselves. I would then whisper this same phrase to them, each and every night, just before I kissed them goodnight: "U can be, do, and have anything U want in this world, as long as U work hard, believe in yourself, and are kind and compassionate toward yourself and other people." We only have eighteen years to pack their suitcases; I wanted to be sure to give them every mindset tool I possibly could.

Make a gratitude jar. This has become one of my daughters' and my favorite traditions. We have a glass jar in my bedroom with notepaper and a pen that rests on top of it. Every now and again, whenever any of us thinks of something or just happens to pass the jar, we jot down something we are grateful for, whether it's the home we live in, the trip to California we took, the good grade one of the girls got on her math test, or the smell of our puppy after his bath . . . anything! We make sure we include the date of the event with each gratitude note. Then, on New Year's Eve each year, we take turns reading through all of the things we were most grateful for that year. We have done it for so many years now and it's something my daughters excitedly wait for, knowing that we will remember wonderful things we otherwise may have forgotten about.

The power of chocolate. Chocolate doesn't talk back. Chocolate doesn't judge your parenting skills. Chocolate understands. Enough said.

Play games. See how U can gamify everything! In our home, boring trips to run errands were livened up with questions such as "How many red cars do U think we can count between here and the grocery store?" And we played games like *Clue*, *Trouble*, and *Categories* ad nauseam. U can even find us rocking out in the car recording our very own "Carpool Car-aoke" songs to this day. I did this when the girls were little, and now that they've grown into teenagers, we still do it. Why? Because technology is brilliant … and … it's a mind suck. Creativity, silliness, and pure, simple fun are harder and harder to come by these days. Challenge your kiddos to think and create while U get to do the same!

For those of U interested in bringing the joy of *Categories* into your own home, here is what our "game board," created by Suzanne herself, looks like! Create your own and make lots of copies to have on hand.

♥	Category	Category	Category	Category	Category	
Letter						Score
Letter						___
Letter						___
Letter						___
Letter						___

TOTAL [   ]

To set up the board: Have your players each shout out five topics (countries, things that are blue, world cities, things with wheels, etc.). Those categories are to be written in the boxes that run horizontally across the top of the board. Then in the column that runs down the left side of the game board, have players choose a letter to write in each space of the left-side column. Any letters will do; some of our favorites are the more common letters: S, R, T, and A, for example. No right or wrong here . . . if U want to up your level of difficulty and throw in a Q or Y, have at it!

Scoring: Players receive twenty points if their answer is completely unique, ten points if they share an answer with one other person, and five points if three or more people have the same answer. U can only get zero points if U leave a box blank or if U get a majority vote of thumbs-down from the other players because your answer simply didn't meet the category or letter criteria. Once everyone agrees that time is up and everyone takes turns reading their answers aloud (laughing all the way), the person with the most points at the end of the game wins!

Helpful hint: Sometimes, an obscure answer is best; other times, the obvious can win U twenty points because everyone else also thinks it's obvious and doesn't choose it. So beware of the mind games that will ensue . . . be clever, defend those creative answers of yours, and, most importantly, HAVE FUN!

About the Author

Jodi Low is an accomplished corporate trainer, an inspirational speaker, and the founder and CEO of the award-winning, heart-based leadership-development company U & Improved.

Jodi has trained tens of thousands of entrepreneurs, Fortune 100 executives, and company teams on how to build a booming business, master a mindset for success, and achieve the lifestyle they desire through heart-fueled leadership. Her series of interactive, performance-based classes at U & Improved covers a variety of workplace topics including leadership, communication, confidence building, goal setting, and trust.

Jodi also launched a teen leadership program in 2014 to empower young adults to become more confident and motivated future leaders. And in 2016, she founded a nonprofit—the U & Improved Leadership Foundation—that makes the program more accessible to deserving teens by offering scholarships for the U the Teen Leader class.

An inspiration to her community, Jodi has received the 2019, 2020, 2021, and 2022 Sun Devil 100 awards for being among the top hundred fastest-growing ASU Sun Devil owned and led companies. In 2015, she was honored as one of the state's Outstanding Women in Business by the *Phoenix Business Journal*. She has received the prestigious Diversity Leader of the Year award from the Diversity Leadership Alliance in Arizona, a Sterling Award from the Scottsdale Chamber of Commerce, and a Silver Stevie Award for Female Entrepreneur of the Year. In 2021, U & Improved was awarded the highly esteemed Torch Award for Ethics by the Better Business Bureau. Jodi is also a highly involved member of the Executives' Association of Greater Phoenix and is actively engaged in St. Vincent de Paul's advisory board.

As a devoted single parent, Jodi and her daughters volunteer countless hours of work in their community through the National Charity League. They are passionate about travel and recently welcomed their newest addition to the family: a Bernedoodle puppy named Cashew. *From Me to U* is Jodi's first book.

IMPROVED
UandImproved.com

CPSIA information can be obtained
at www.ICGtesting.com
Printed in the USA
JSHW080734201122
33330JS00001B/7

9 781610 661010